The Wonder of Play

The Wonder of Play

Explore its magical connection to learning, self-motivation and well adjusted kids.

Author: Stephen Andrews
Illustrator: Cindy Farmer
Publisher: Camelot Printing, Inc.

The Wonder of Play by Stephen Andrews
Illustrations by Cindy Farmer

This book was typeset in Myriad Pro, Myriad Pro Light, Caveat, Mom I Love You So Much, and Gill Sans MT

The illustrations were created using pen and ink, and Prismacolor pencils

Interior Design by Stephen Andrews
Author Photo by Marc Laucks
Writing guidance by Sarah Galbraith Laucks

Published by
Camelot Printing Inc.
7634 Lafayette Road
Lodi, OH 44254
330-242-3772
EarthSongFarm.com
DisccoveryParkOhio.com

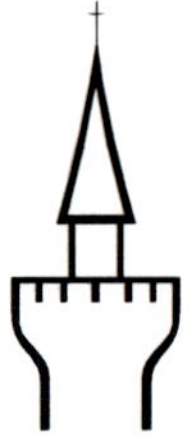

There is inherent danger in reading this book.
It is likely that you will never see play
the same way again. It may also revive the desire
for play in you and not just the kids.
This may have unintended consequences
in any current relationships.
Please take it with a sense of whimsy, as there
may be long-lasting side effects!

979-8-9916154-0-2 - Paperback
979-8-9916154-1-9 - Hardcover
979-8-9916154-2-6 - Ebook
979-8-9916154-3-3 - Audiobook

Dedication

This book is dedicated to kids. It's dedicated to parents, teachers, and grandparents. When you understand play, you will never grow old (even though your body may wear out).

Be Inspired - Regularly

As you read this book, I know you will be curious about a playground that captures kids' attention and enthusiasm for hours. So many kids have said as they leave Discovery Park, "This is the best playground ever." So here is a link to that playground: www.DiscoveryParkOhio.com

I also randomly write a newsletter to share ideas with parents and grandparents about how the short time they have with their children can have more depth (and fun). If you would like to read some past issues to see if this appeals to you, go to **www.DiscoveryParkOhio/Blog.htm**

Here are some past titles that might intrigue you:

Touch my Heart
I Love My Cell
My Accidental Job
The Summer Slide
I'm Expecting
Where is Yoda when you need him?
My Feet Wanna Dance
Treasure Maps

Thousands of parents who have visited Discovery Park receive these newsletters, and they must be of value since I usually have at least a 40--50% open rate, which I've been told is outstanding. I write when God tells me to write. He usually gives me a title first, and then, when I grab my clipboard, the words just start flowing. I'm just a vessel.

If you would like to receive these random newsletters, go to https://tinyurl.com/38askjf

We never share or sell this list and you can unsubscribe anytime. I know you're overwhelmed by too many emails already, but this may have value for you.

Thanks, Steve

Preface

If you interact with kids, you need to read this book! YOU played when you were a kid. You looked forward to the day's adventure. Even though we played outside in the winter, we couldn't wait for spring and summer.

Play is potent. When a kid plays, he is discovering his world. He is figuring out how everything works and how he is to participate in it. Play is the most powerful learning technique ever!

Too often, we fail to realize its power and think it is something we should grow out of. **WRONG**. When you recognize the power of play, you want to use it, even as an adult.

Today, a kid was visiting our homemade playground for the first time. He said, "This place is even better than Cedar Point Amusement Park." He was right, but he didn't understand why. For over three hours, he climbed, ran, and explored. That discovery process is what play is all about.

I have had a passion for play all my life, subconsciously. But in 2019, I decided to test my ideas by building a three-acre playground. Some of my ideas flopped, even before we created them. We watched intensely as the kids explored every nook and cranny. My sense of play has grown to the point that I know what will work even before I design it. I can tell you which activities will even engage the adults in play.

Let your imagination run wild as you explore every page of this book.

As I have studied play and how kids learn, two authors stand out in my own growth. Dr. Peter Gray wrote a masterful book called "Free to Learn."

John Holt's three books are: "How Kids Fail," "How Kids Learn," and "Learning All The Time." John spent many years teaching 5th-grade classes. He observed how the school system worked from the inside out. He was deeply disturbed by what he saw. His first two books have sold over a million copies and been translated into 14 languages. He became so disillusioned, that he initiated conversations with parents to take their kids out of school and start teaching them at home.

Intro:

This is the intro to a book I haven't written yet. I do things a little backward from how most people think it should be done. The first step is for us to get connected. I am not a researcher in the ways of academia. My research is reading extensively and observing over 10,000 kids as of 2024 who have visited the playground that my wife and I started building in 2019. Ideas flow to me – constantly. Discovery Park Ohio (our playground), was an experiment. Could we create a space that was so fun that kids wouldn't want to go home? Could it be a space that continues to challenge kids as they grow?

DISCOVERY PARK

As you have probably already noticed, this book is artistically designed. You are welcome to jump around and experience this book in any way you would like. **There will be no tests. There are no gold stars.** Remember your own childhood play. Let your imagination go. Play is not just physical; it is also an attitude, a mindset. Being playful with your kids and spouse can happen at any moment. One of our biggest surprises when we built our playground was that it was so much fun that even the parents and grandparents jumped in and started playing on everything too. What a joy to watch!

This book explores the stages of growth, physical and mental, and observes how it shows up in play. We will explore the different ways we see the world and how play helps us work out our understanding of the world as we interact with it. The book's second half delves into how play is connected with the learning process.

This book is your cheat sheet. In it, you will discover new ways to understand play, your kids, your partner, your parents, and even yourself. MARK THE BOOK UP! Circle things that impact you. Underline phrases that stimulate. Make notes in the margins so you don't forget ideas. Don't just read it. Absorb it and let it transform your life and the short time you get with your kids.

The Learning Process

Although this book's primary focus is on the importance of free play, play is also the basis for how we most easily learn. Discovering how to learn is critical to life's success.

Learning tip: Don't reread or highlight. Read a page, turn to the next page, and mentally recall and summarize the previous page in your own words. This forces the brain to move that info from temporary storage to permanent storage in your brain. You have just "owned" it!

Hand powered railroad

A"maze"ing

A real airplane

Wobble

Windup

DiscoveryParkOhio.com

FORWARD

Most of us would agree that children are truly delightful beings. Two of the most gratifying states in which one can observe them are deep in sleep or joyfully lost in play. As a teacher with 20 years of experience and a certification in Waldorf education, as well as a mother of four children aged 18 to 4, I find that this book aligns with everything I've come to understand about children and how they thrive. While I joke about the sleeping part (though it can feel like a small miracle), the importance of child's play is no small matter.

Whether it's an epic battle among a four-year-old's toy action figures, an eight-year-old happily humming a tune while perfecting a drawing, or a group of children bursting into a lively game of tag after finally settling on rules in a meeting as serious as a UN summit, children are at their happiest, most engaged, and eager to work when in their natural state of play. In "The Wonder of Play", Steve and Cindy share their genuine passion for helping parents shed confusion and empower their kids. Let's face it: empowering kids to play is something that only the best teachers occasionally land upon.

In today's educational landscape, the term "schooling" can be confusing. The Wonder of Play helps families seeking a more autonomous path grapple with questions like: Do we pursue homeschooling? Find an alternative school? What about unschooling? Is that really a thing? And what about the self-doubt that leads many of us to question whether we are qualified to be our child's teacher at all? When I first ventured into homeschooling with all these questions in mind, I felt an overwhelming need to control my child's experience, burdened by high expectations.

In the following pages, Steve offers insights into the power of teaching critical thinking and helping children shine as the inspired, creative beings they are. He highlights the diverse ways in which we learn, explains why kids push boundaries, and discusses the value of facing new challenges and engaging with peers of all ages.

This book invites you to trust your child and become their guide; to celebrate curiosity and perhaps rediscover your own ability to play. I encourage you to explore the insights within and embrace the journey. Trust that there is freedom in allowing our children's passions to shape their daily experiences—free from rigid agendas.

Enjoy!

Carrie Burchett
October 2024

Have You Lost Your Play?

At what age did you lose it, 8, 9, 10? Did you decide you were too old for playgrounds, or was it peer pressure? It could be the type of playground! You probably don't remember going down your first big slide. It was scary at the top of the ladder. You wanted to go back down the ladder, but there were other kids climbing up. No choice. WOW, that was scary and fun. It was almost like flying.

All the older kids are riding bikes. "How do they do that?"

Some Things Can't Be Taught

Play and being playful creates joy. Even in a relationship, playfulness creates excitement – the unexpected. A playful spirit creates joy and smiles all along its path. Instead of staring at the sidewalk or your phone as you walk, say "Hi" to others and smile. You just changed the mood of that person. Put some "genuine energy" into it. Try skipping or put some dance in your walk. People will watch and be thinking – I want what she has! They may even come over and become real (physical) friends.

Let's go back to the question of why you lost your play. It may have been because the playground was no longer challenging. You've done it all. The swing was fun when Dad pushed you, but he got bored. You wanted to continue, so he showed you how to "pump it". Got it! Higher and higher. Then you tried jumping out. Next, it was standing up. Then, it was two on the swing simultaneously (facing each other). Finally, you ran out of ideas. You have pushed the limits of that experience. You've even done "things" you weren't supposed to do. And every swing is just another swing. That's how it is with play. As soon as it is no longer a challenge, it's time to move on.

You wanted another adventure, but the typical playground wasn't a challenge and didn't satisfy your curiosity and sense of adventure anymore, so you moved on.

Culture arises and unfolds in and as play

~ Johan Huizinga

Play is Powerful!

If you think back to your earliest memories, they were probably about playing. The truth is, we all instinctively are driven to play. That's great!

Babies are instantly curious. They somehow know that their mission is to understand everything they encounter. If you hand a simple object to a baby, they immediately grasp it and start exploring it. They taste it – not milk. They feel its texture with their tongue and study its shape. What color or pattern does it have? Is it heavy or light? Is it shiny or dull? Even though they don't understand all these qualities yet, they are little scientists, recording everything possible about this object. Is it warm or cold? Does it make a sound when I shake it? Finally, they will decide that they know all about this object, throw it down, and find a new object to explore. It is so amazing to watch them discover.

They are building a mental/visual database in their mind. Everything in their world is new and ready to be explored. As their mind builds this mental construct, they recognize items and want to play and explore with some of them more. Within the first four years or so, they absorb unbelievable skills and knowledge without any instruction. Imagine if people could continue to learn at that rate their whole life.

They learn to crawl, walk, run, jump and climb. They are learning how to control this body vessel they were born into. "How do I make those things at the end of this appendage move or wiggle? What does this taste like? WOW, that was sour! What is the meaning of the sounds I am hearing? Can I imitate those sounds?" They learn to understand and speak the language of the home they were born into. And soon, they will assert their will, argue, amuse, annoy, befriend, and ask questions - relentlessly! They absorb an incredible amount of information about the physical and social world around them. Does this depend on someone teaching them how to learn this stuff? It's all natural. They want to know through their instinctive playfulness and curiosity. When they turn five or six, this curiosity doesn't diminish. They want to keep learning at that same pace.

Whoever wants to understand much must play much

~ Gottfried Benn

To play with a child is to love a child

~ Vince Gowmon

What are your earliest memories of play?

___

___

___

___

___

___

___

___

Stages of Play...

We often forget that a child's mind develops neuron connections every moment. As the mind starts forming these connections, it can gradually understand the world they were born into. Each child has to go through definite stages of mind growth. Although the length of each stage can vary and the transition from one stage to the next can be erratic, they still must go through these stages. We tend to focus on the external: are they standing, walking, and talking. However, the internal growth of the mind may be even more critical.

These stages were shared by Richard Dettner, AIA, in his book "Design for Play," written in 1969, on pages 24 through 30. The book may be old, but the stages remain the same.

From birth to two years old, play is pretty solitary. Babies will want to engage in play with older siblings as they gain skills in walking and balance. They want to be just like them, so they will push themselves to be in more control of their body and to understand what is being said. They use many non-verbal cues to understand the world and the interactions. They are in the phase called "practice play," which includes repetition and pleasure as the cause of an external event.

An example is picking up an object and watching it fall. Do it again – same result. In a sandbox, they may use a shovel, fill a bucket, and then dump it. They may do this again and again. If there is a puddle, they will jump in it repeatedly, watching it splash out. Peek-A-Boo is the beginning of recognizing that just because I can't see something now doesn't mean it no longer exists. The joy of Peek-A-Boo is contagious. The squeals of delight are so powerful and happy.

2-4

As children move past the two-year-old point, they are still growing rapidly and daily learning how to control their bodies. They are learning the meaning of words, both spoken to and spoken from them. There is an early understanding of symbols. I no longer have to point to a carrot when I want one. I can say "carrot" (word symbol), and mom will get me one even if I can't see it. The child is now moving into symbolic play - commonly called make-believe or pretending. A stick can be an airplane, a truck, or a boat. He will be moving it over his head if it is an airplane. They can become so absorbed in this imagination that surrounding kids seem invisible. They may play side by side, but their actions are only loosely connected or interactive.

4-6

Moving past the four-year-old stage, we move into the intuitive stage. This is where a young girl starts to organize her experiences. Logic is still not a strong point. Instead, she relies on intuition to determine what feels right. She is full of questions as she goes through this stage for a couple of years,. Why, why, why? She is trying to match her intuition of the situation with the reality. (Or maybe she knows her "whys" bug you, and she just wants your attention or a hug!) She is refining her mental picture of the world. This will eventually build a concept of logic that she can trust as her mind develops.

In play, she will significantly enjoy interacting with other kids. Some play may be an imitation of others. Although she knows there are rules to be followed in some play, her logic skills haven't developed to keep track of them. She will change the rules on a whim. Now, she has to deal with conflict with others who disagreed with her rule change. Now she's upset, frustrated, or outright angry. Everybody quits and starts a new activity. That may be easier than resolving the conflict. This world of social cooperation and mutual understanding is challenging to maneuver through. Realize that working through these issues is the power of free play. **Do not interrupt these conflicts.** There will be anger, crying, and frustration. Let it happen! They have to learn how to resolve conflict and handle their internal emotions. Mom and Dad stepping in steals that life skill that is developing.

7-10

As a child moves into the seven-to-ten-year-old range, his mind develops the skills needed to follow rules, use logic, and anticipate outcomes. He can unravel a situation and work backwards to see how a change may affect the outcome. He is eager to engage in play with others, and they can work together. He is mature enough to understand other people's points of views and can work with them. Games with rules are exciting, whether playing with partners or in competition.

The world around him is no longer strange, but he wants far more depth of understanding. Abstract reading about the world isn't good enough. He wants to feel it, smell it, taste it, and listen closely. Nature fascinates him. Go for a hike and catch bugs, smell wildflowers, pick leaves to identify, and dig in the dirt to see what is happening underneath. How deep do roots go?

He wants to know how everything works. Give him some tools and old appliances. He will be thrilled in the disassembly.

11 - 15

Finally, we get to the 11 to 15-year-olds. For approximately four years, their ability to think like an adult is developing. He can project the consequences of his actions. He can develop theories and test them. He can mentally form complex situations and evaluate all the options. He still enjoys play; it is just far more thoughtful, not just running around. If he runs, he wants to know how fast he runs. Can he run the same path tomorrow and be faster? He may be taking on adult roles if allowed. Although he may have chores like mowing the grass, shoveling snow, washing the car, taking the dog for a walk, or even cleaning part of the house, these are all practice experiences for the adult world. As he gains and improves these skills, he may start doing odd jobs for neighbors and earn some of his own money.

*Stages of Play is the most important chapter in this book. Each child must go through these stages and the stages will overlap. **DO NOT** try to rush this process. Let it happen naturally. So, look back at each stage and summarize them in one sentence.*

____

____

____

____

____

____

For Older Siblings

When you have kids going through different stages, it can be confusing. The transition from one phase to the next doesn't have clear markers. As a parent, you may notice the changes in desire or understanding. This will not be so obvious to an older brother or sister with younger siblings. They are immersed in their own development. Even though they went through these stages, they probably don't remember them. Spend time talking to any older kids about what happens in each stage and help them understand why that pesky little brother or sister wants to hang with them but can't keep up or "cheats" when playing a game. Not only will it smooth out the relationships, but it will also help them decipher how the world works.

Understanding these different stages will also give them insights into the parenting skills they will one day need. Girls will probably understand this sooner than boys. They usually have more compassion and can understand the differences better. Soon, they will also learn, just as you have, that not everyone thinks the way you personally do. This is also a tripping point.

When I was a kid, I wanted to explore and build things. My brother (three years younger) never wanted to run around in the woods. He just wanted to immerse his mind in the fantasy worlds of fiction books. To this day, you would never guess we are brothers. We live in entirely different worlds and have totally different values. Yet we accept each other as we are.

We need that understanding to be positive people living in a crazy world. It has been said that the most essential life skill is **how to work with other people.** Play gives us chances to explore that negotiating and understanding role.

The very existence of youth is due in part to the necessity for play; the animal does not play because he is young, he has a period of youth because he must play

~ Karl Groos

If you have multiple age kids (that's most of you), write their name and stage below. As you think about their stages, how can you help them understand the stage their siblings are in. Take the time to talk with each one individually. Do this each six months. They are all moving up this growth path.

Example - Joey - 5-years old, wants to play ball with his 8-year old brother. Joey doesn't understand rules and can't control his muscles very well. But he wants to be just like his brother. Such motivation!

How Kids See Play

What is play? The word is used in many ways, but we will focus on how kids see play.

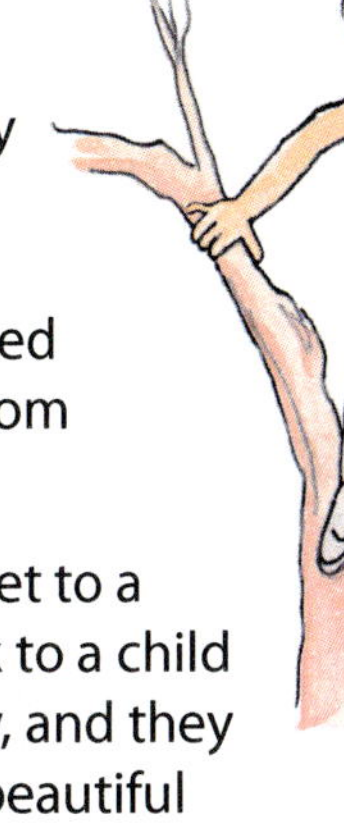

Dr. Gray, who has studied play for most of his life, discusses the essence of play in his 2013 book "Free to Learn." I have paraphrased and condensed his ideas from pages 139 and 140.

Play is not serious, yet to a child, it is serious. Talk to a child immersed in play, and they will share beautiful insights about the excitement they are experiencing. They use all their imagination and can change things spontaneously. Yet play has rules and resembles the real world. Through play, children and many other animal species learn how to navigate and succeed in adulthood.

In more primitive cultures, throwing a spear, tackling a wild animal, or starting a fire are all play, but they are also real-world skills that are being honed and refined. We think of it as childish. We need at times to force ourselves to see the world through their eyes at times to understand the picture that we may have become blind to.

Here are three general points about play that we must remember.

1 Motivation and Mental attitude. Two people might be throwing a ball, pounding nails, typing on a computer, or baking cookies. To tell which is playing, you have to study their expressions and attitude. Take a professional ball player. When he is lobbing some balls to kids on a neighborhood ball field, he is playing. When he is throwing a curve ball and getting a strike, we may call it "Playing Ball", but he is hard at work. Is the cookie baking for the family picnic or are we making hundreds to sell in a bakery?

2 Second, it doesn't have to be all play or not play. Play can blend with other motives and have a little of both. If someone is being "playful" at work, they may be trying to stimulate you to a deeper level or get you out of a rut. Even writing this book is both. I love sharing **my** understanding of play, but it is work to try to organize it and say it so that you will grow from this reading.

3 Third is not neatly defined. Look for 5 key elements:

1 Play is self-chosen and self-directed

2 The activity is more important than the result

3 Kids make up the rules, but they can change whenever they want

4 It is about imagination - not reality

5 The kids are active and alert but not stressed

The more of these traits that are visible, the more likely it is called "play".

Different Types of Play

Physical Play

Kids need to develop strong bodies and refine their coordination. So they engage in physical play, including running, leaping, chasing, and rough and tumble games. Children, on their own initiative, don't run laps or lift weights to get in shape. Instead, they chase each other around, wrestle or have play sword fights. They will play until they are exhausted and do it all over again later in the day.

Language Play

Nobody has to teach language to young children. They learn it on their own. First, it is vowel oriented cooing sounds like ooh-ooh. Then it changes to babble sounds as they combine consonants and vowels for ba-ba-boo-ga-da-da. When a baby is happy, these sounds start to flow. It's self-motivated for the pure joy - not to get something. All these sounds fit the definition of play. At about one year the first words start flowing. Soon, they will make phrases and then full sentences. Then comes the vocal fun of rhymes and puns and silly word combinations.

Exploratory Play

The need to figure things out is strong. They are little scientists studying how everything works. This is part of the mental map they are creating of their world. Why do apples fall? This curiosity can continue for a lifetime if no one squelches it.

Constructive Play

Learning about our world also leads to wanting to participate in its construction. Let's build a sand castle. How about a spaceship from these old boxes. The size may be big or small.

Constructing may also be language based, such as telling tall fibs or stories. Maybe they want to put on a play or write their own book. Did someone sing a brand-new tune?

Fantasy Play

Just because something doesn't currently exist doesn't make it any less real. Kids say, "I put a handle on a small box, and I'm going to work. When I get home, I can tell you all about the adventures I had or the stress I was under." It's play, as much as dressing up like a princess or fighting the dragons. This is also the development of logic as they try to visualize what is happening and what comes next.

Social Play

Kids want to play with other kids as they grow. Learning to interact with others is a powerful skill. Kids enact roles, but who gets to play what part? What are the rules of this game? What role is each player taking, and what happens if they don't follow "the rules"? This takes negotiation, which everyone has to agree to, or the game falls apart. Nobody wants that, so the strong-willed child gets outvoted and has to play fairer if he wants to stay in the game.

All these interactions are happening simultaneously. They just do it, and you have to pay attention if you want to see it in action.[1]

Nothing lights up a child's brain like play

~ Dr Stuart Brown, M.D.

Children at play are not playing about.
Their games should be seen as
their most serious minded activity.

~ Michel de Montaigne

Play is the highest expression of human development
in childhood, for it alone is the free expression
of what is in a child's soul

~ Friedrich Froebel

What kinds of play do you see your kids involved in? It is important for you to look closely at this issue. Each of your kids are developing their own personalities. Only if we let go of what we want them to be and let them discover who they are, will the joy of life blossom. Write down what kind of mind you think is developing at this stage. Later, you can look back and see if that is the path that actually developed. Some of your kids may have more than one trait, write them all down.

Play is Freedom

Play is what one wants to do, not what one is obligated to do. I'm sure you can relate to that idea as you think about getting off work on Friday. Play is voluntary. If someone said you have to go play now, and you were in the middle of reading a great book or deep into level three of a video game, it doesn't feel like play.

The joy of play is the ecstatic feeling of liberty. It's not always accompanied by smiles and laughter. Sometimes a tongue hangs out in concentration or a deeply furrowed brow. Likewise, smiles and laughter are not always a sign of play. It may have just been a good joke. But play always has a sense of YES; this is what I want to do right now. They have chosen this moment or activity. If they are playing with others, it also becomes the most accurate form of **democracy**. Whatever the game, they want to keep it going. Do we need a leader, lets vote. He's doing a lousy job; try someone else. If the rules aren't working, let's figure out some new ones and come to an agreement. If no one can do the give and take, then the fun stops. Nobody wants that. If someone tries to bully others, we walk away and start a new game without the bully. Play is such a powerful way to learn how to please others without displeasing yourself. Sometimes it may even lead to a mini brainstorming session of trying to figure out what might work for everyone.

Adults trying to participate in play with children is very difficult. Adults are always seen as authority figures in a child's mind. For them to become playmates is hard to imagine and even harder to do. If a conflict arises, the kids will look to the adult for a solution. Most adults assume their adult role and offer a solution. To stay in child mode as an equal is hard. To look at the kids and say, "I don't have an answer. What do you think we should do?" They might then consider you an equal - maybe. The role of an adult in the play space is like tightrope walking. It's possible, but failing is likely.

Consider this! Kids are playing. You want to build a rapport with them. I'll just join in. You step in. Suspicious. Adults usually want to take control because they think that is their right as an adult. Game's over, we all walk away, or maybe we have a bit of pity and let you play for a little until we all just walk away. But if you genuinely understand play and can be simply one of us - not trying to be in control, but just as a participant for the joy of it - then that's OK. Continue the game.

If an adult initiates "play," it may be fun if I have the choice to participate. If it is not my choice, then it is not play.[2]

Think about work. If you have a lot of freedom about how you do your "work" and there aren't deadlines, then it may feel like play. If I can also start and quit whenever I want and no one is judging my work AND I love what I'm doing, then it very much feels like play.

This is the real secret of life—to be completely engaged with what you are doing in the here and now. And instead of calling it work, realize it is play

~ Alan W. Watts

Play is the exultation of the possible

~ *Martin Buber*

Children need the freedom and time to play. Play is not a luxury. Play is a necessity

~ *Kay Redfield Jamison*

If animals play, this is because play is useful in the struggle for survival; because play practices and so perfects the skills needed in adult life

~ *Susanna Miller*

Motivation is Everything

Why we do things is important. If we work because we need money, or run because an angry dog is chasing us, it obviously doesn't feel like play. The goal is the paycheck or outrunning the dog. What is important isn't the journey, it's the end. **Play is the opposite.** The goal isn't the end but the fun of the journey. I'm not counting how many times the swing goes up to break some record; I'm enjoying feeling the air rushing by and the sense of weightlessness at the end of each stroke. I pedal my bike because it takes me someplace else. It doesn't matter where; it's the fun of pedaling hard and coasting, going up a hill and the feel of the wind as I go down a hill. Today I feel creative and since there is no traffic, I make wide sweeping curves or ride with no hands learning to steer by just leaning slightly. What fun!

In play, I study deeply because I want to understand how something works, not because there is a test. But that research led me on a different path that looked interesting, so I studied something else. I get tired and stop. Tomorrow, I will continue this exploration. It's fun, and that makes it "play". Think of a kid drawing a picture and coloring it. He doesn't expect it to hang in a gallery, although it may get put on the refrigerator. It really doesn't matter. It was about expressing an idea that he had in his head and seeing how accurately he could bring that idea to life. It's about his discovery, not a show. Even though there was a goal of completing the drawing, the result was not having a finished drawing but the fun of doing the drawing.

If there is a competitive game going on with points being scored, to a child, the fun is getting good enough to get a point. It isn't about me getting more points than the other team, although someone may point that out and somehow claim that makes you better than the other person. Does that really make you a better person? Play isn't about competition to compare skills but about gaining the skills alone.

It's time for some self-reflection. What are the motivations that are guiding your life?

RULES There are mental rules in Play

I had never thought much about play having rules. Play has many rules. But most of us never notice these rules. It's like body language. A person makes a joke about us. Ouch. But then they smile or wink. OH - they're teasing or flirting. We have learned these subtle body language signals our whole life, but it is subtle. We don't think about it, and probably no one has taught us these clues. The same happens in the world of play.

Play has hidden rules that the participants follow. Given a pile of blocks, a kid mentally envisions what these blocks could represent. They don't end up being another pile of blocks over there. They turn into a castle, a house, a battleground of tall trees and hills. If another kid comes over and starts using the blocks, too, he has to agree to the original concept, or there will be conflict. Either the conflict gets resolved, or they will build two separate visions.

If kids are play fighting, they don't use all their force when throwing a punch. They know it's just a game and what the rules are. You don't actually hurt the other person, or the game will end, and anger will break out. Not good. We want to continue playing, so we mentally play by the unspoken rules.

A complex rules-based game is set up when kids decide they are going to "play house". Who is the mommy. Who is the dad? How do we work together and resolve issues? Do we have kids, and what about a dog? There are lots of rules that are being worked out, just like real life. If someone doesn't abide by the rules, then there is conflict that has to be resolved, or no one will be happy. The complexity can actually mimic real life.

When the father figure says, I'm exhausted; what's for dinner, he may actually be tired of trying to keep track of all the self-generated rules.[3]

A child who does not play is not a child,
but the man who does not play
has lost forever the child who lived in him

~ Pablo Neruda

People tend to forget that play is serious

~ David Hockney

Have you ever considered the hidden rules in your life? The alarm goes off on Monday morning. Do I stink and need a shower? What clothes are appropriate at work? How will I deal with the annoying person at work? Can I really say that to my boss? Will I get pulled over by a cop for not making a complete stop?

Hidden rules: ____

____

____

____

____

____

____

____

____

____

____

____

____

____

____

Let's try an experiment:

Not all Brains are Alike

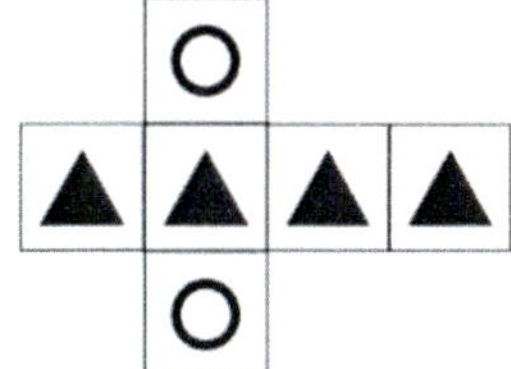

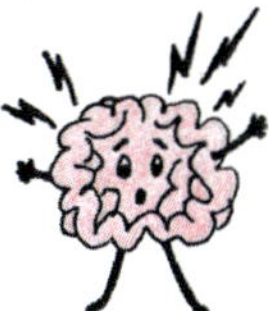

Which cube cannot be made based on the unfolded cube?

A 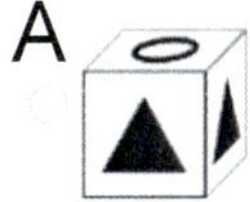 B 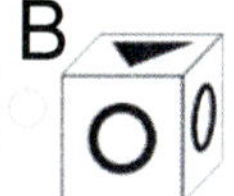 C  D 

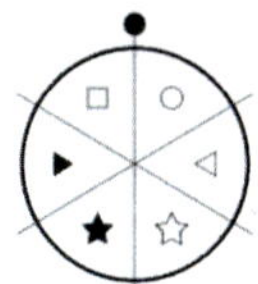

Which figure is a rotation of the object?

A 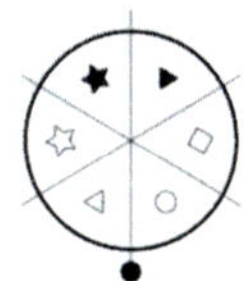 B 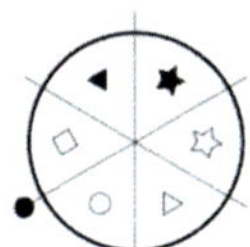 C  D 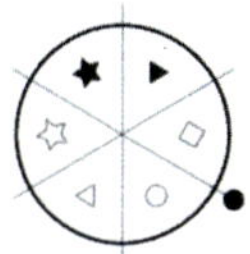

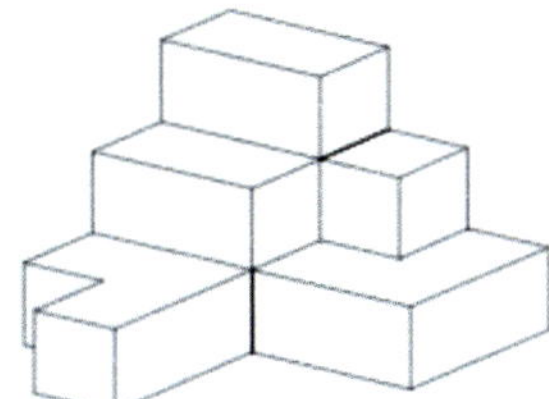

Which figure is a top-down view of the given shape?

A  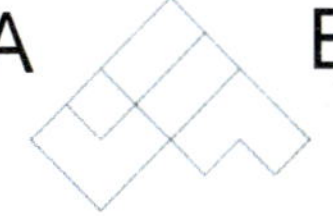 B  C 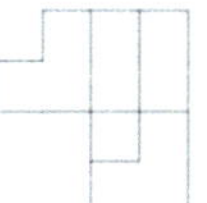

D  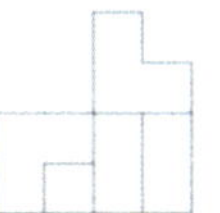

Turn the page

Answers

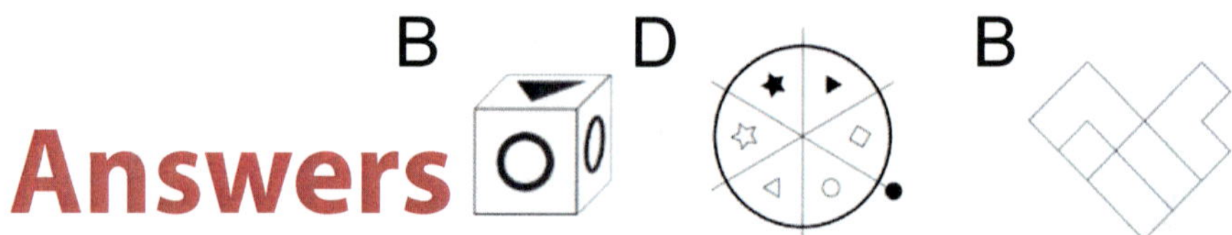

If you struggled to determine the correct answer, you probably don't have a mind that thinks 3 dimensionally. That isn't bad; it's just different. Professions that require 3D thinking include engineers, architects, and sculptors. Although the brain stores information visually, our society is so heavily dependent on the use of words that most people think with word symbols. Those who really get into word smithing often are authors. There are many ways that the brain processes information. As you study those around you, and especially kids, you may see a predominance in the way they live their life.

Obviously, your kid's minds haven't developed yet to the same level as an adult's. However, there may be something bigger at play than you realize. Our brains aren't all wired the same.

In my senior year of high school, I took a drafting class. I got straight A's. I couldn't understand why other kids also didn't get A's. It was so easy! When I went to college, I applied to be an Architecture student. That's when I discovered why drafting was so easy. I had a 3-D mind. Most people don't.

Schools are primarily based on "word smith" brains – processing and using words/symbols effectively. But many kids struggle because words are not how their brain works. Let's look at some different types of brain "processing."

Undirected play allows children to learn how to work in groups, share, negotiate, resolve conflicts, and learn self-advocacy skills

~ Winnie Wathu

Your kids don't think like you!

WordSmith

They can create a scene in your mind that dances with life by using the right words that connect with your soul. They love reading and are already writing children's stories or maybe starting their first novel.

Music

Vibration is everything – how to make it, work with it, enjoy it. It's more than listening to songs. They sing; they drum the table... every instrument has to be tried. They create their own songs and turn everything into sounds.

Competitive

Games are everything. It is not so much about winning as it is about the challenge. Competing on a field or a screen, alone or on a team, it's always the challenge.

Analytical

Why, why, why? Never happy with a simple answer, they want to know in detail why the sky is blue and how bread rises. What causes the wind? Why do flowers bloom?

Body Movement

They're always moving – dancing – gesturing – running. Their whole body wants to connect with the world. They feel the beat, or they create their own beat. Their body becomes an instrument to express their inner feelings. They don't just follow a lesson; they create what feels right. They run and jump, honing their skills. Controlling the muscles and bones is exhilarating!

Grower

Connected to the earth. They are passionate about plants, soil, weather and their connection. They talk to the plants, and they can hear the plants talk back. Every season brings new joy and discoveries and they want to understand how plants can grow even in the winter.

Intuition

They know. They can't explain it; it just comes to them. They know what will happen next, what someone is thinking. Their insights surprise people, even themselves. They are deeply reflective of life and their sensitivity to body language helps.

Inventor

Their natural curiosity guides them to explore everything. Their mind is constantly asking, “Is there a better way?” The mind is continuously thinking, watching, interpreting. They can't shut it off.

Problem Solver

Born to fix things. If it doesn't work, they will make it right again or better. They spot problems easily and are eager to try to resolve those problems.

Compassion

They see the world through the eyes of others. There is a heart energy at work. They may sense an animals' feelings. They love everybody they meet because they feel their energy.

Builder

Hammers and tools, 3D printers, clay, steel or cement. All are items that can be manipulated and worked with to create. Even girls who want to sew or love crafts are included. Creating something new is their passion.

Artist

Study the flow, colors, shape, and movement. No matter what media, an artist is passionate about communicating with light and vision. They can visually compose a scene so a sense of depth is pulled out, and the colors all work to create a striking design.

3D

Does your mind visualize a building just by looking at the plans? Can you turn that building around in your head and know what the back looks like too? You are mapping the world as complete images, not just flat pictures.

Taste/Smell

The nose and mouth are supreme. Smell every flower, and everything has to be tasted. They know what's for dinner by the smell. They want to cook and try different seasonings and they love gardens and flowers.

All our minds work differently. You may have strong energies in just one of the above. You can paint a beautiful picture, but someone else has to make the frame. You may be a generalist and have a variety of skills and interest areas. If you're a specialist, you want to know everything about a certain area. You are obsessed with that area and go way deeper than other people. That's OK; it's just the way you are wired. Just keep in "mind" that just because this is the way your mind works doesn't mean your kid's mind works the same way. Nor does your spouse, best friend, co-worker, boss - that's what makes life exciting!

Part of these differences can be loosely related to the brain's two hemispheres. Although this is still an unproven theory because of the complexity of the mind, many believe that the left side of the brain is stronger at logic and mathematical

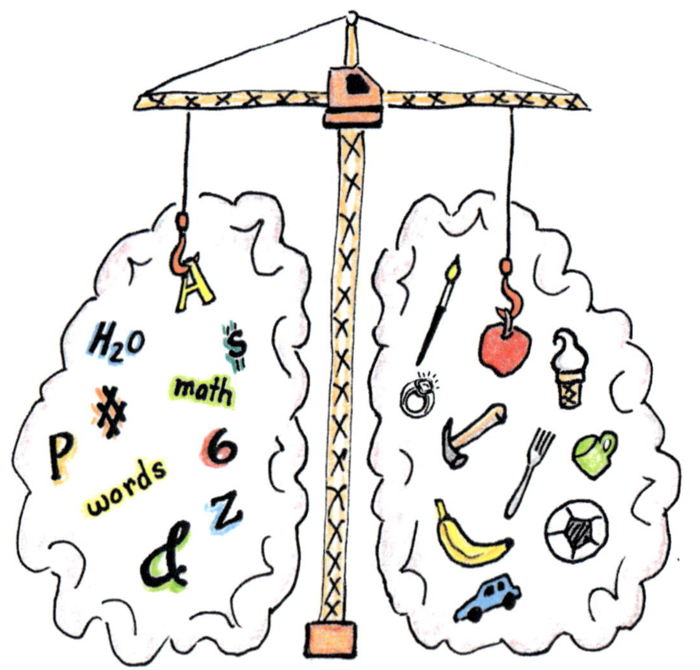

constructs while the right side deals more with creativity and the what if. A left brain dominant person might end up being an engineer or an accountant while a right brain focused person might be an artist or a composer. It's not that it's all or nothing, just as you may be right-handed does not mean your left hand is useless and just hangs by your side. You can use both. It's just that one hand seems to do things easier. The same way with the brain. Just because you love to sing doesn't mean you can't make change at the grocery store. Suppose you are working with kids that seem really different in the way they are processing information than you do. It may be because they **really are** processing info differently.

A left-brain predominance allows you to turn concepts into symbols that you can remember and manipulate. The right-brain person is mapping the whole universe in 3D in their mind. This takes longer, so they are often considered to have learning issues. In reality, they don't have a problem, it's the person evaluating them that doesn't understand how this kid's brain is working. They may fall behind when they learn to read or do math. Don't panic. They will eventually decide that their brain is comprehending the rest of their life journey enough that it is now time to do something called "reading." If allowed, they will quickly catch up to their peers and even surpass them because their life is more focused on a passion for discovery.

I'm betting you've been evaluating your own brain's style. So, write down what resonated for you.

One final example.
If I say visualize an apple,
what do you think of?
Turn the page.

If this is the image that popped into your head, you are probably left-brain predominate. Your brain is storing symbols, like a short hand for the real thing.

If this is the image that popped into your head, you are probably right-brain predominate. Your brain is mapping everything in detail. You are asking what color of apple, does it have a bruised spot, and if there are any worm holes on it. You are painting a picture that is as realistic as possible. This will slow you down, but it's just your way of understanding the world.

I had two interesting conversations recently.

One person said he couldn't read a drawing, but when he had a hammer and nails, he just knew what to do and his structures came out beautifully.

A repair man for my printer said he could take a complex machine completely apart and come back a week later and put it back together perfectly. But he admitted that he was a horrendous speller.

Conflicts in Play

Play with others is going to involve conflicts. As kids play, this is normal. **This is actually great.** When there is conflict, they have to resolve the conflict, or the game ends, and everyone is unhappy. Negotiations start happening. They don't know what that concept is, but they are doing it. You broke the rule. Are you going to be punished or forgiven? Why did you break the rule? Are you sorry or do you think you had a right to break the rule? Should we modify the rules? Everyone has a say. Those with the stronger argument will probably sway the group. If that person is just being demanding like a bully, they will be ignored until they come back in line with the rest. It is actually wonderful to watch this happen. But don't interfere. **If you step in as an adult, you've just robbed them of learning how to get along with others.** They are learning a life-long skill that will help them later and teach them what makes a good leader.

When they reach a consensus, it doesn't mean they all agree. It just means that everyone will go along for the opportunity to continue the game. Again, a great life lesson. It's about practical reality. You don't always get your way and if you insist on it, you will be playing alone.

There are times when there is more negotiating going on than actual play. Great. They realize that learning to work together is an integral part of playing together, even if it is a lot of work to come together. That negotiating skill is a life lesson that will continue long after the game ends.

Which team will I end up on?

I remember playing baseball on a vacant lot. I was always the last one picked. Nobody really wanted me on their team, but they also didn't want me just sitting in the grass, watching. "Maybe he'll get better today." I probably didn't. But they were kind enough to put up with my strike outs and missing the perfect fly ball. Dr. Gray talks a lot about the contrast between informal games and organized sports on page 101 of his book "Free to Learn."

There is really no difference between your team and the opposing team in play. When kids break into two teams to play a game, they know it isn't permanent. The idea of our team being better, is not important. The next time you might be on the other team. The group decided that your skill was needed on their side because you could help make it a more even game-playing process. Maybe you could help pass on some of your skills to the other kids or maybe you're just good at team building encouragement. Nobody likes to look foolish or be on the losing team every time. Kids sense that and try to constantly adjust the rules and teams so it becomes as even as possible. It's no fun playing a game if certain teams are always the same and always win. Who wants to bother playing?

Let's look at a sandlot baseball team. Nobody is a pro. They are all learning how to get better. Maybe there aren't enough players to fill all the slots. One kid becomes the catcher for both teams. Maybe the emphasis is on hitting the ball. The best pitcher is always on the mound because he knows how to help each player practice their hitting by sending just the level of pitch that will challenge, but not overwhelm. He's not on a team, but he may be the most important player because he makes the game fun by varying the pitch to the level of each batter.

When it comes to play, discovery and practice are far more important than actually winning. When you go home and tell Mom about the ball game, you're going to talk about how many times you hit the ball. You're going to talk about the technique another kid taught you about how to swing the bat or catch the ball. Who won the game really isn't important. It's about the fun we had playing the game.

Deep meaning lies often in childish play

~ Johann Friedrich von Schiller

Your family has conflict. It's never ending. Let's try a new tactic, "The Socratic Method." First, you don't have the answer and if you did, it would probably be wrong! Bold statement - right. In the Socratic style - always ask a question. Only by continually asking questions can we drill down to the real issues.

"Mom, I don't want to go to bed." "Why not?" "I'm in the middle of building this amazing Lego City." "Can you build it to a certain point and finish it tomorrow?" "Probably." "At what point will you be ready to call it quits for the night?" "How about when I finish this building." "OK, call me when you get it done. I'd like to see it."

Each kid will react differently, but you are turning the tables on them and forcing them to solve the issue instead of just demanding blind obedience. Eventually they may start using this technique in their own lives when they have conflicts, even when playing with others.

Think of an example of what your child might typically ask. Instead of giving them the answer, what questions could you ask to get them to figure it out?

____

____

____

____

____

____

OK - you tried it. It probably didn't go well. That's to be expected. Everyone expects you to just lay down the law and grumble about it. You changed the rules of the game. Keep doing it. After awhile, the whole family will catch on and start doing it too. The family will start moving deeper than the surface interactions and irritations to find what actually is the problem.

When each person starts to realize their own actions are affecting others, then change will be easier. This will also give them a wonderful tool to use through all of life's problems. Just don't start a blame game. That's when defenses go up and change will be nearly impossible. "I have to defend my position, even if I know it is wrong. My pride is at stake."

The effect of mixed ages in play

Mixed age play helps kids grow. I watch this "Play" out every day at Discovery Park. There are kids helping each other put the trains back on the track. The older kids teach the younger ones how to balance the wobbly merry-go-round. It's almost as if everyone is "no age".

Kids on a playground don't care about what age you are as long as you want to play in an equal way. In that sense, even adults can participate as long as they don't misuse their "adultness". Age mixing is actually a secret weapon that allows kids to develop quickly and in a balanced way.

Let's assume you are the youngest in a group. You look up to all these older kids. You want to be like them, so you watch carefully and mimic their actions as closely as you are able. Good playmates take the time to help you be a part of the action. They want you to succeed because that makes the game more fun.

As the oldest playmate, the games may be boring. You've already played this game many times and know the ins and outs that allow you to succeed. So it is no longer as challenging to you as it is to the younger kids. But you stick it out because you want to be a part of the play-group. Your focus now shifts to helping others learn how to play more successfully. You help each kid at whatever level they may be, to improve their skill level. Because you are one of them and not an adult "teaching" them, they are more readily open to your ideas and suggestions. It's a win-win.

Those in the middle ages are also learning from the older ones because they, too, are looking up to them. If you are in that middle group, you are experiencing both roles, being taught and encouraged by the older ones and sharing tips to the younger ones. Everyone is improving their skills, which makes the game more fun. If everybody was the same age or level of skill or understanding, none of this cross interaction and encouragement would be happening.

I was lousy at playing ball. Now imagine that my best friend was also lousy at playing ball. I throw the ball - wildly. There is no way he can catch it. He throws it wildly at me, and there is no way I'm going to catch it. This is no fun. Let's introduce an older kid who is better coordinated at throwing. He tosses me a ball in a way that I can practice catching it. I throw it wildly back at him, and he practices catching those wild balls. He then throws the ball to my friend while I study how he performs that feat. My friend catches it and throws it wildly back. This is fun! We're all learning a skill and having a good time too. As we get better, each of us ups our skill level and learns to not be so wild, but maybe faster. In the meantime, the kid doing the skilled throwing challenges us with more difficult throws as he sees us getting more skilled. Because the older or more skilled child does not see himself as an adult or coach but just having fun, he doesn't judge the interaction or make it into more than it is. We're just having fun.

Give childhood back to children:
if we want our offspring to have happy,
productive and moral lives,
we must allow more time for play, not less

~ Peter Gray

In play, a child always behaves beyond his average age,
above his daily behavior. In play it is as though he were
a head taller than himself

~ Lev Vygotsky

Take the Green Pill

"Look deep into nature and you will understand everything better."

~ Albert Einstein

It's not your fault, but it is your problem. **Kids spend an average of 30 hours each week watching TV or computer screens. Outside activity is averaging only seven minutes a day.** As a consequence, childhood obesity has skyrocketed. The sedentary nature, and junk food are slowly killing the ones you love. It's not just weight but cardiovascular disease, stress, sleep issues, and more.

Free play is increasingly recognized as an essential component of wholesome child development. This kind of play not only exercises their body in a tremendous variety of ways, but also stretches the mind. Even something as simple as hide & seek, tag or riding a bike is powerful.

As adults, when someone mentions "stress", we assume that it only refers to adults. But often, kids are under even more stress! The stress comes from school assignments, friendships and bullies, getting along with brothers and sisters, and not feeling like you have much control over most of your world. The world we are living in is full of stress, which is directly linked to emotional and physical health issues. So, don't miss the point that Einstein refers to above.

Get outside and into nature, daily, if possible. Research has shown that being in the natural world has proven health benefits for all ages. It's more than just sending the kids outside. They need to see **YOU** valuing the connection to the natural world. They need to see you being wondrous about the beauty of brilliant fall leaves, a fresh layer of snow, the flowers pushing up in the spring, and the warm sand between your toes at the beach.

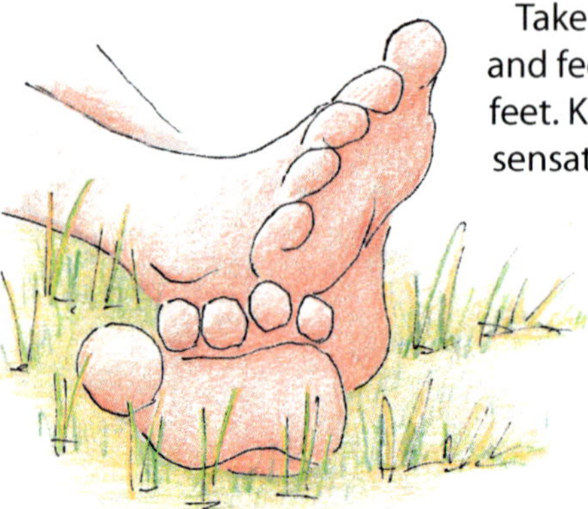

Take off your shoes when you can and feel the cool earth under bare feet. Kids love being barefoot. The sensation of cool grass, squishy mud or sliding on the morning dew is exhilarating. Being barefoot actually pulls free-radicals out of your body which will improve your health. When was the last time you were barefoot outside other than the beach?

Winter doesn't change your need to be outside. Yes, you stay in when there is a hurtful wind chill, but winter is also beautiful. Don't dread it! Learn to dress for it and take the kids for a walk in the freshly fallen snow. Feel the flakes on your tongue. Look at the sparkles of the snow in the sunshine.

My dad hated winter. He finally moved to Texas and thought I would also move there. But I learned to dress for the seasons and relish the wonderful variety. Having animals on the farm forces me to go out to feed them every morning. There are days I'm not thrilled – pouring rain, driving snow. But once I get with the animals, my mood changes. Some days I just sit with them, and they gather around for attention – even the hens and roosters. I wouldn't trade that connection for any fancy resort. Every day I am outside, connecting with that day's gift. Even in the barn, I am connected with nature. I feed the animals hay which still smells of summer. A scoop of grain that was lovingly mixed to keep my animals healthy. It all came from nature. When February comes, so do newborn baby "kids" (goats). The wonder of watching them stand for the first time on their little shaky legs as they naturally know to look for mama goat's udder is amazing to participate in.

Let's take a walk at the local park. Remember that kids are in it for the adventure and not the end. If you never make it more than 100 feet into the woods, that's OK. Just stop and sit. Let the kids explore "off the path.' At first, they will see some trees. OH - I hear a bird singing, and I feel a cool breeze coming out of the woods. The longer you sit in silence, the more they will discover. Do they hear a bullfrog in the distance? Can they smell a flower or some fragrant "weeds"? Are they picking up a leaf and trying to determine what tree it came from and what type of tree it is? If you hear some water, go down to the river bank and let them explore along the edge or even into the shallow parts of the water. Take a bug box in case they want to take home a bug for further exploring. Although this isn't seen as play, it is. Quiet, exploratory play is just as powerful as noisy running play. It's all about discovery on their own terms. If they want to wade in the water, let them if it isn't deep or fast. If it's the edge of a swampy area, that's even more fun because that's where the best bugs and frogs can be found. You never made it to the end of the trail. Who cares!

Look in your own backyard. Is it, or can it be made into a space that would be great to have adventures in? Can they build something with some old lumber and nails? Can we put blankets over the swing set and make it into a campsite? Can we take a telescope up to the top of the slide platform and be on the lookout for Indians? Give them a floppy hat, a cheap compass, and a magnifying glass. They are suddenly explorers. Hide some old bones in the sandbox and let them be archaeologists.

Don't miss a chance to model for your kids what it means to be connected to the "real" world, not the digital version. Check out the website – 1000HoursOutside. It will challenge you to walk away from the screens and hold hands as you walk out the door!

HEY KIDS! What adventure shall we take today?

I wish I could hear about all he adventures you had. Yes, some didn't go as planned, but that may make them the most memorable.

I remember our first family camping trip when I was a kid. We found a beautiful site in a Michigan campground. We set up our trailer/tent combo. Mom and Dad on the trailer top and each of us on cots. It rained, and rained, and rained. The stakes in the sand weren't long enough to support the downpours. The tent was collapsing and then hail came down!. Finally, dad walked through the freezing water and put us kids in the old Rambler car for the night. Yes, a very memorable disaster we are still laughing about.

What adventures will you take?

____

____

____

____

____

____

____

____

____

____

____

____

____

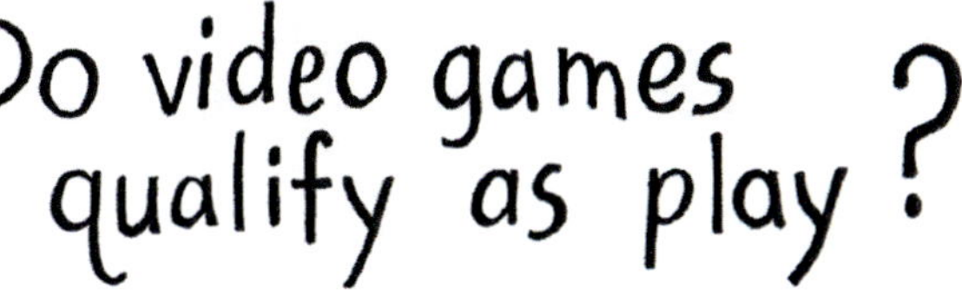

"My kid's addicted to video games!" Really? It may not be as disastrous as you think. In many multi-player games, there are instances of real leadership skills being required. Often, games use teams of people, and someone has to lead the group. What a great way to learn and practice leadership. At some point, you also have to convince other players that you would make a great leader. It's like a job interview. This is a good way to develop introspection and skill set evaluation. If you lied about your skill set, you'll quickly be discovered and ousted. Better for this lesson to be learned in a game than the hard reality of getting fired from a real job.

YES. I know this is controversial, but kids who play video games and also have access to the outdoors will find a balance. The key is: do they have access to free play outdoors and is it considered valuable by the family? If your choice is playing video games indoors or going outside to be intimidated by bullies or drug pushers, video games may be the better choice. But given a safe outside experience, most kids will choose to be outside, especially on a beautiful day. If they have some friends riding bikes on the street out front, sure, they're going to want to join the fun. But there are days when it is raining, windy or cold. No one else is outside. So they settle into their favorite video games.

All is not lost. In a sense, they are just playing with imaginary friends. If it's an online game, they may be interacting with kids from all over the world and maybe learning things from their culture. Many games require a team effort, which requires negotiating and strategy work. Of course, they are also gaining hand eye coordination and maybe being able to think and analyze quickly so their airplane doesn't get shot down or their buddies don't get ambushed on the battlefield. Kids also love fantasy, and this helps them broaden their fantasy concepts from simple to complex. Maybe you're worried about all the killing and screen violence. Kids can differentiate between what is happening in a game and the real world. It won't make them into killers but might actually sensitize them to the value of life.

Do not trust the age level recommendation of the manufacturers. They keep lowering the age level on the package to increase sales. Some games are truly gruesome and evil. Choose wisely - with your kids. Help them understand that even games can be "programming your mind" with unhealthy things.

There are also simulations that can teach them city building, being a battleship captain or a train engineer. When computers first came out, I took one with me when I visited a nephew. He had never experienced a computer before. I showed him a few basics and then loaded up Microsoft Flight Simulator - version 1. By the end of the day, he could fly every plane and land perfectly at every airport. I know he crashed a lot, but that's part of the discovery. He could go back and replay what happened and analyze what he did wrong. He later became a pilot and is flying commercial airplanes to this day.

People rarely succeed unless they have fun in what they are doing

~ Dale Carnegie

What is addiction? I love chocolate. If I don't have any for several days, I'm not going to have withdrawal symptoms. So that isn't an addiction. Video "addiction" may be similar. Find a balance with screen time. Talk with your kids about screens not being the real world but can still be worthwhile. Go for an agreement of five hours per week (negotiable). Put it in writing and make a chart for the fridge. Let them track their time. Two hours today, none the next, and one the next day. Time management - self taught. Let them even design their chart! The more they are invested in the idea, the better the chance for success.

Dangerous Play

"Better a broken bone than a broken spirit."
~ Lady Allen of Hurtwood

Kids deliberately put themselves at risk! They climb high in trees, dive off cliffs into deep lakes, and jump from rock to rock. Even little kids throw pillows on the floor and jump from couch to pillow, and another pillow because the floor is "pretend lava". It isn't truly dangerous at this point, but it is make-believe danger. On a traditional playground, kids will get bored quickly and start doing things they "aren't supposed to," such as climbing on the outside of the equipment or going up the slide. They perform tricks and have playful fights. The stronger partner will self-handicap, so the weaker kid can break free and keep the game going. Have you ever had a bunch of little kids pile on you - the monster - and try to take you down? You know they aren't trying to hurt you, so you go along with the play, tossing them off as they squeal with delight.

Think of how many games are "chasing games". The little girl screams as she is chased by the "monster". She's running from her father, who threatens to "eat her for breakfast." What fun! In the chase scenario, the one being chased is in the preferred position. They are constantly looking back to make sure the chase is continuing. If she gets caught, now she must be the "chaser".

Almost every game you can name is basically a variation of tag. Football, basketball, and soccer all have a bunch of people chasing each other around. It's you against a horde of wild people. Even baseball has you running, chased by other players or having the ball trying to "catch" you.

This combination of fear and joy we call thrill. Kids are testing their prowess. How high can I swing? How high

> can I climb? Can I swing from this rock "across the river"? Fear is being challenged, but not terror. Nobody is forcing you to do something against your will - that's terror. You are challenging yourself, your current skills and your fortitude. To not allow that kind of play is frustrating to the child. "I know I could have done it, but now I'll never know for sure."[4]

We seriously underestimate children's ability to take care of themselves and make good judgements. **Even good judgements that fail are great learning lessons.** I watched one kid go down the slide at Discovery Park on his belly and land on the ground. It knocked the wind out of him. He just laid there for about 45 seconds and then turned over and announced, "I'm never going to do that again". Another lesson learned.

As parents, we need to trust the process. The helicopter parent destroys the child's ability to test their skills and judgements. It is far better to learn what they are capable of when they are young than to suffer those failures as adults. Our goal as parents should be to give them the skills they will need to function fully in their own adult life. It is not our job to teach them how to live and tell them what to do after they become adults. Let them play and test their abilities as a young person!

We are never more fully alive, more completely ourselves, or more deeply engrossed in anything than when we are playing

~ Charles Schaefer

Play builds the kind of free-and-easy, try-it-out, do-it-yourself character that our future needs

~ James L. Hymes Jr.

Adventurous Play

Adventurous play is initiated by the child. He sets the rules, plays as long as he wants, and quits anytime. He is not trying to achieve some end result. It's just the joy of exploring and imagining.

A parent's role is to provide a rich environment that encourages this discovery process. A good environment may include a home, yard, nature center, or park. Adventurous play is challenging. **The child is testing his skills, overcoming fear, and trying new ideas.** Adventurous play allows for lots of ways to do something. Nothing is the "one" right way. Adventurous play should involve some calculated risk - a challenge. It's not dangerous, really; it's just a little scary. As children test and practice their new skills, it becomes less frightening.

Did you ever swing on a rope to jump into a stream or a lake? Did you ever cross a gully on a fallen log? Did you ever try to jump over something, and didn't make it? Write down some of your adventures and mishaps. Someday your kids may read this book when they have kids. They're going to see this page and say, "You really did that?" A smile and a twinkle will break out on your face. "Yep!"

Most of our discussion so far has been about active play. But there is also a lot going on with quiet play. Quiet play might be with dolls and dollhouses, superheroes, and monster trucks (although that might get a bit noisy)! As children grow, they are eager to take the knowledge of their world and turn it into their own fantasy time. "I have to feed the baby, and then it's nap time." "My superhero has to save the world," as we jump from the dresser to the bed and onto the floor. They become the characters and envision themselves being the mommy, the superhero. At younger ages, this is solitary or with a stuffed animal friend. Interacting with another person will bring conflict. As the child matures, another playmate brings excitement and challenges as you play your part, and they play theirs. They are practicing the skills they see around them. Many families have a play kitchen or workbench and can see the role-playing going on. They will talk with imaginary people, serve tea to the stuffed animals, and spend hours creating worlds out of Legos.

Quiet play is just as powerful and necessary as active play. As a parent, you must provide room in the daily schedule for this quiet time. Building a hideout in their bedroom with ropes, sheets, and clothes pins is creative and calming. "It is my hideout from the world." It's a place to contemplate the day, think about the fight with your brother, read a book, or fall asleep. This quiet play is essential to growth. A TV show, a video game, or a busy schedule gets in the way of this incredibly important time.

As they mature, the concept of rules starts to develop. If Chutes and Ladders was one of your first board games, raise your hand. It's a simple game based almost entirely on chance – you flick the spinner and start moving your piece. It takes two to play. Conflicts happen. You can't go up the slide! You were supposed to go 5 spaces. A lot is going on here. Working with numbers and moving your piece in the right direction. How important is winning? An older playmate may want to win (ego), the younger is just enjoying the process.

PUZZLES

Remember wooden puzzles? First ,you start with the cow shape, which can only go in the cow hole. Then comes 24-piece puzzles, 100 pieces, etc. Obviously, you don't give a toddler a 500-piece puzzle. They'd eat the pieces.

Puzzles are very good play activities. At first, it is shape recognition and learning to turn the piece till it fits. As the difficulty increases, the child learns to look for other clues like color, one straight edge, three knobs – not two. Puzzles are also an excellent family activity. It is calming and quiet but can also lead to great conversations. They can learn that their mind can be both fitting pieces together while talking and listening.

ARTWORK

The old coloring book. Did you have a coloring book? How many hundreds of pages did you color? How many crayon colors did you have? Did you also have colored pencils or watercolors? There are many elements of quiet play going on here. Scribbles came first - "Look, I created something." Then we practice hand/eye coordination to stay within the lines. We're also learning the proper colors of the world – trees aren't purple. As the child's skills develop, don't just get a more detailed coloring book. Give them blank paper and challenge them to create their own world. Continue their growth by introducing new art materials. Go beyond the flat, 2D plane and start working with 3D items like Play-Doh. Remember that kids don't always think like us, so our role is to encourage, not evaluate.

GAMES

After the child is capable of playing by rules, a whole new level of quiet play opens up. It may be card games like Go Fish or Yahtzee. These games are still based primarily on chance, but strategy is starting to arise. This requires the deeper level of thinking we discussed at the book's beginning. Checkers are simple to play with few rules, but they also helps you develop strategic thinking skills and the ability to anticipate what your opponent might do. It can be easy to play for beginners who are often fascinated by just moving their pieces around. Remember that it isn't about winning; it's about participation and strategy. I've seen many boards shoved off the table when a game was lost. Good time for a talk concerning the joy of play rather than the outcome. A similar game is Connect 4.

Continuing down the development path are more complex games. Twister is unique. Not only can several players play at the same time, but its focus is not on strategy but on agility. It is great indoor exercise for any age on a rainy day or at a party.

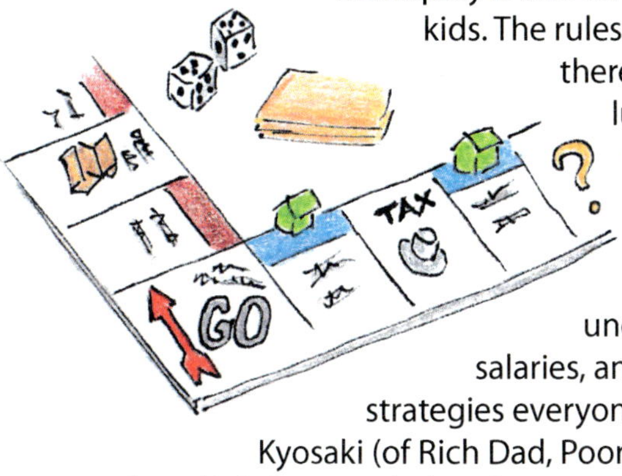

Monopoly is also an excellent game for older kids. The rules are pretty simple, and there is a lot of randomness and luck with the draw. But the strategy is the important part. Kids are learning how to work with money, investing, paying rent, unexpected expenses, and salaries, and keeping an eye on what strategies everyone else is using. Robert Kyosaki (of Rich Dad, Poor Dad fame) said his best friend's father taught him how money works by repeatedly playing Monopoly. (Robert's own father was a professor and always broke.)

Scrabble is another great family game for older kids. It challenges them to see words in a random group of letters. But it's more than that. Bigger, harder words get more points. Then trying to fit it on the game board utilizing your letters to get even more points. This is way better than spelling tests.

You probably get that quiet play is just as powerful and satisfying as active play. Good activities challenge kids but aren't beyond their level of maturity. Quiet play is also a strong family bonding experience. Color with your kids. Let them watch you blend colors and add things to the coloring page that were not printed there. Soon, they will try it, too. As a parent, **just remember the rule about free play – I can quit anytime.** You may actually rediscover the joy of coloring. Your level of focus may be much longer than your child's. Let your child move on when they want. Their hands and fingers may be getting tired. Also don't think you should <u>teach</u> them these techniques. Just do it and let them see what is visually unfolding. If they imitate your technique, then it becomes their skill.

In our play we reveal what kind of people we are

~ Ovid

Children have always learned and created places for themselves through play

~ Donna R. Barnes

When China entered the US market, inexpensive plastic toys flooded the shelves. Many had bright colors, flashing lights, and sound effects (great for battery makers). But now kids have so many toys in their bedroom that there is little room to play with them. Mom tells them to clean up their room, but it is a daunting and overwhelming task that often leads to meltdowns. I still remember the day I was given such an ultimatum. I tried, really tried. But after hours of trying to figure out where to put everything, I gave up. Part of the problem was I started playing with the toys instead of cleaning. Finally, I just scooped everything up and threw it in the closet. That is not exactly what Mom intended.

Here is a time-proven way to reduce the "toy" issue. Get a box and a trash bag. If the toy is broken or has missing parts, put it in the trash. Whatever is left, have your child pick out their six favorite toys (negotiable). Put the rest in a box. Yes, there will be protests. Think of the box as a toy lending library. × Brilliant Put the box on a high shelf – not in their room. When they get bored with or outgrow a toy, they can exchange it for one in the lending library box.[5]

The problem is that when there are too many toys, a child will spend a few minutes with one of them, then on to the next and the next, never really staying with one experience. They are flitting, never able to focus. But watch what happens. When you limit the toy choices, they can more easily pick one toy and focus on true "play." letting their imagination take over. That is what play is about.

Many toys are often a waste of money, and too many toys do not lead to actual play. The real toys have staying power because they encourage imagination and challenge. They don't do just one thing. They allow the child to change it, invent a new way, or idea. It is involving all of their senses. The toys' beauty is they keep challenging them even as their mental abilities expand. Legos are the most successful toy ever made. But maybe your kid isn't a builder. Get them a quality art set, a microscope, their own sewing machine and leftover fabric. They may have a fascination with reptiles or small animals. Get some. Get some real tools, scrap lumber, and build a small workbench – together. I still remember asking Santa when I was 11, for a "real" drill. My dad's drill was a piece of junk, and I loved to build things. You can't believe my joy when I got my first, real, quality drill.

Kids are looking for reinforcement. "Look at me, look at what I can do!" They are asking for your understanding and participation in their new skill levels. They seek approval. Even though their mind may not be processing like yours, they need to be assured in their journey.

Children don't need more things.
The best toys a child can have is a parent
who gets down on the floor
and plays with them

~ Anonymous

Pets

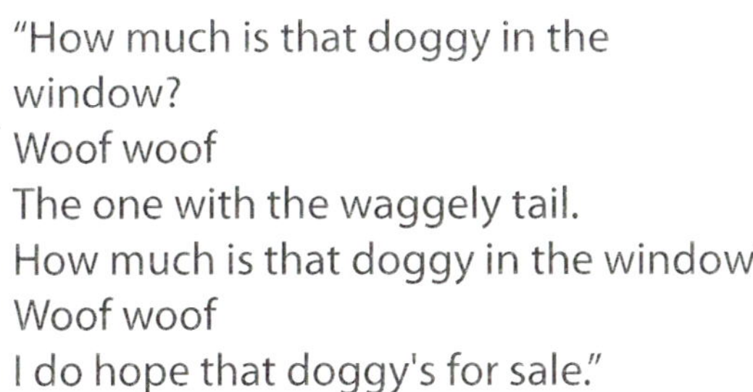

"How much is that doggy in the window?
Woof woof
The one with the waggely tail.
How much is that doggy in the window?
Woof woof
I do hope that doggy's for sale."

A popular novelty song written by Bob Merrill in 1952 and first sung by Patti Page

(Did you sing the lyrics?)

There is an element of fantasy in pets. They are cute when they are a puppy or kitten. There are promises of "I'll take care of it." In three months.... guess who is doing all the chores? So, how do pets end up in a book about play?

There are times when pets are a great choice, especially if you live in a suburban or rural area where there aren't a lot of other kids around. A dog or a cat can become a surrogate playmate for an only child. They may also become a tremendous source of comfort, someone to snuggle with. But it is still tricky.

- **Will the breed overwhelm a child as it grows up?**
- **Is it a type of dog that likes to be around people?**
- **Is it low maintenance?**
- **Will it be confined to a small space or only be kept inside or outside?**

These questions apply to cats, too.

Personal experience: We had a dog when I was growing up. It was a Toy Fox Terrier that loved my mom and wanted nothing to do with the rest of the family. It was a yappy 4-pound dog that slept whenever he wasn't barking at some unknown sound. He wasn't much of a companion to the three of us kids.

When I started my family, we got a flat-coated retriever puppy that maintains its puppy-like playfulness throughout its life. It is considered a medium-sized dog that grows slowly. My son loved that dog. When we first brought him home, he knocked my two-year-old son down and climbed all over him as he licked my son's face. My son was in ecstasy! They grew up together and did everything together. He has had many of the same breed over the years and now has two of them, along with his 5 kids.

A good pet choice, cat or dog, can make a great play buddy. They can romp through the woods, wade in a stream, and chase each other all day until they are exhausted and curl up together under a tree. Even a cat can stay playful when grown, if you take the time. The important point is the companionship between the pet and your child. I'm sure other animals can be playful, but look at the long-term picture. We have 6 kids right now (baby goats are called kids). They are so much fun to watch and interact with as they run and jump. But they would not make much of a pet long-term as a substitute playmate.

It's time to name your pets. Remind yourself what was great and not so great about each one.

BOREDOM

"Mom, I'm bored." We've all heard that and probably said it to our own mom.

"So, what do you find boring?" Helping a child to figure out what is causing their sense of boredom is the first step to finding a solution. Our goal is not to find entertainment or diversions for them. Boredom often comes from being entertained by TV, video games, etc. Turn these things off and let them be bored. After you have figured out why they are bored together, it is time to start finding a solution. Teach them the idea of "Brainstorming". Write down every possibility of things to do you both can think of. Don't evaluate each idea. Just write it down. When you have exhausted ideas, go back and evaluate what might be fun to do. Put an asterisk by each one. Then, let them prioritize what they want to do first, second, third, etc. You are helping them see that life has many possibilities when they climb out of a rut. If they don't cooperate with that idea, let's go to step two: Let them be bored.

Within a day and a half, they will start creating their own play experiences. They need that boredom to shift gears. The same happens to us. We get into a rut and finally can't stand it anymore. We don't have mom to complain to, but we suddenly start figuring a way out of the boredom. Unfortunately, we often replace the boredom of being entertained with doing something else that is also entertainment, like going shopping, a ball game, going out to eat or going to a bar. None of these will ultimately satisfy that boredom because it is just changing to a different type of entertainment, which will also lead to boredom. Are you bored with going out to eat? Have you tried every restaurant in town? Maybe it's time to take a cooking class.

To shake off the boredom, you must let your mind get free of the everyday routine and start creating.

Do something you've never done, like writing, journaling, painting, drawing, biking, hiking, camping, sewing, or anything that puts your mind in a fresh and creative mood. Maybe you will find a new passion! The same needs to happen with kids. Changing the type of entertainment isn't going to solve the boredom issue for long. Let them be bored. Let them beg for you to intervene. **Don't!** That boredom will eventually lead to creative play.

There's a flip side to boredom - over commitment. We're just trying to pack too many activities into our day, our week. There are opportunities that may come unexpectedly to us, but we have to turn them down because our life is already too packed. Let's list our weekly obligations:

I know you saw this coming, but look back at each obligation and ask, "Do I really want to do this?" Cross it off. You need a schedule that can let the unexpected enter. When you hear yourself saying, "YES, I want that," then you have the room in your schedule. Don't give in to the "That might be nice."

Play that isn't Play...

Organized sports are **not play.** Sports may have value, but does a child want to participate for the right reason? Too many kids are more stressed than we are because of all the activities they are involved in. We drive them to private lessons, team sports, gymnastics, soccer, baseball, ballet....They're exhausted, and so are you. Do they say yes to all these activities because they fear disappointing someone by saying no? Are they saying yes because they want to please you, and are you pushing them into it? Are they saying yes because all their friends are doing it, and they want to be with their friends? Most kids want to have free play time – no rules, no deadlines, no practice, no performance and no pressure.

As parents, we often feel the pressure to keep our kids on the path to sucess. We want them to have a good life and be independent. However piling on advanced classes and after-school activities doesn't necessarily lead to a successful life. The pressure to get into a prestigious college doesn't guarantee happiness. We'll delve into this a bit more later on. But for now, it's important to remember that excessive pressure can be counter productive.

Loving the exploration of life is far more important than achieving success. Besides, what is important today may have no importance to the world they will be living in. When was the last time you had to use trigonometry to determine the height of a tree? When did you last look up a word in the dictionary or use the file cards at the library? Most of us can't even remember how to figure out the area of a room or the multiplication tables. After all, we have smartphones that tell us anything we want to know. The real skill is in learning how to ask the right questions.

Here is an essay about informal sports as they are played at the Sudbury Valley School. Michael Greenburg, a former student at the school, presented some revealing thoughts about kids playing sports.

> "In all the years of playing very physical games like football, soccer and basketball at Sudbury Valley, there has never been an injury beyond a minor cut or bruise. People play all these sports in their regular clothes without any extra protective equipment that is normally required. How can this be explained, when people wearing protective pads injure each other with alarming frequency? Because, in a regimented, performance-oriented way of looking at sports (or life), making sure you don't hurt someone becomes less important than winning. So, it doesn't matter how much you talk about sportsmanship or how many safety pads you wear, people are going to get hurt.
>
> Alternatively, when you approach sports (or life) as a fun, exciting process, as something that is done for the sheer joy and beauty of doing it, then not hurting someone, not impairing their ability to enjoy the same process, becomes a top priority. To participate in an activity where the clash of unequal bodies is transformed through teamwork, pursuit of personal excellence, responsibility, and restraint into a common union of equal souls in pursuit of a meaningful experience has become one of the most profound experiences of my life. I am sure it has had a similar effect on others."[6]

Contemporary Playgrounds

Every community has playgrounds, many of them. Every elementary school has one.

If you look past the bright colors and arrangement, **they are basically the same.** A platform you climb up to with stairs, rope net, or slanted "rock wall." Then you peek through a few holes or a fake telescope, spin a plastic ship's steering wheel that does nothing, and then slide down a short slide – maybe straight, maybe curved. There are some springy things and a few swings with short ropes. If you are three or four, this might be exciting a couple of times, but where does the challenge to push kids to grow physically and mentally?

Each playground costs $100,000 or more, and then there is landscaping and installation costs. It may be an insurance company's dream, but where is the challenge of encouraging our children's development?

From a kid's perspective, a playground should be open-ended in how to use the "equipment". Does the environment provide challenges and testing of skills? Does it silently tease one into exploring the unknown – something I've never tried before? Do I have to evaluate the danger involved and how to stay safe and have fun, too?

A good playground has challenges that keep kids interested even as they grow and develop new skills and understanding of life. Last year, I couldn't do that, but this year, I can! The excitement of discovery is also important. Are the challenges too obvious, or do I just have to "play" with them until I figure out how they work? The child's curiosity needs to be fully engaged.

A playground that is "more dangerous" is actually safer. "How can that be?"

On a commercial playground, kids know that it was all designed with safety in mind, so they don't evaluate the safety aspect of what they are doing. Out of boredom with the standard equipment use, they start inventing new ways like climbing to the very top of some shade canopy.

On an adventure playground, kids can see that there is a chance of getting hurt. They study the situation and determine

how to play on this unique playground without getting hurt. They obviously don't want a trip to the hospital with a broken arm, so they evaluate their play more closely. Every study has shown that an adventure playground is safer than a commercial playground.

So What Makes a Good Playground?

Free play requires choice, not just what ride I want to go on. Amusement parks are "entertainment". You have little control over the ride. At best, you might have a lever that makes your rocket ship go up or down. Then there is the chance to drive a real car - gas pedal and steering wheel. Soon, you realize you're not really in control because there's a track down the middle of the road that keeps you on the roadway.

Ask a kid who has been to Discovery Park Ohio, and he might describe it like this:

"A good playground has activities that I am in control of. I can pump water and install barriers that guide the water or make it activate something. Or maybe a rubber duck can go down the stream. I can see pollywogs swimming in a pond - maybe I can catch some. The slide has no level part at the end. It just dumps me out about 2 feet in the air. At first, I always fell, but now I know how to "stick" the landing.

On the railroad, I can make my hand-cranked car go fast or slow, choose which track to switch onto, and even hook cars together with couplers to make a train.

There's a maze that has three levels. Every level has different activities and paths. There are bridges over a center strip where kids are riding pedal cars underneath the maze. One bridge is held on by chains. At first, it was scary, but now I just run across it. There is a rope bridge and even a trolley that can take me from one side to the other. There's a fire pole and barrels to crawl through. If I take the most challenging path, there is a bell to ring to tell everyone I made it.

There are lots of pedal-powered go-karts of all sizes. One big tricycle has no handlebars. You have to steer by just twisting your body. Even my mom tries riding that!

I love the music area. I get to try out the drums, a xylophone, A pipe organ made of plumbing pipes, and even a Caribbean steel drum.

There are zip lines that I can 'fly' on. A wobbly merry-go-round that not only spins but also goes up and down. About 20 of us can ride at the same time! There's a giant stand-up teeter-totter that a bunch of us can get on and bounce the people on the other end. I love the circular swing. Four of us can fly through the air all at once. But I must tell you, be careful of that little circle hanging from a pole. When you wind it up and jump on, hang on tight or you'll fly out onto the ground.

I almost forgot. There's a real fire truck we can explore. My buddies and I pretend we're going to a fire and are ready to jump out and save someone from a burning building. There's also an actual airplane - up in the air. IT MOVES! I feel like I am really flying it. Move the yoke and it will tilt and climb. Maybe I'll be a pilot someday. This is the best playground ever!"

So, a good playground fires up the imagination and offers lots of choices. The kids experience fantasy, teamwork, choices, and challenges. Although some might think it would get boring after a while, it doesn't. There are always new friends to meet and have adventures with.

Today, a mom said her kid was afraid of heights. At first ,he just watched the other kids up on the maze. Then he tried it and made it to the first level. An hour later, he wanted to do what the other kids were doing further up. He made it to the top. His mom was ecstatic. He was overcoming a significant fear! DiscoveryParkOhio.com

Murder, kidnapping, pedophiles, shootings, accidents – it's everywhere and out of control. Or is it?

When I was growing up, our family took long vacations. I remember laying on the ledge behind the back seat and waving to the people behind us. The idea of seat belts and child seats hadn't been considered yet. My baby sister sat on mom's lap next to dad. There was lead in the gasoline and no airbags. We often stayed in campgrounds and took off to explore while Mom and Dad set up camp. When I was 15, we went to the New York World's Fair. Dad said to meet the rest of the family at this location at five o'clock for dinner. I was on my own in the midst of tens of thousands of people on a hundred acres – no cell phones.

At home, we played unsupervised in the woods and subdivision streets every day. Sometimes, we would walk a mile to the corner store along a busy road with no sidewalks. Was the world that much safer back then?

NO, I don't think so .... Ask your local policeman if the murder rate in your community has gone up. Ask them if child abductions are typically caused by family members during domestic disputes. Ask them about the accident rates in your neighborhood. There may be more crime from burglaries nowadays, but that is probably related to drug use. The chance of your kid being snatched and held for ransom is probably close to nil.

What has really changed is the media and the Internet. Sensational stories are what people read. If you read or listen to that sensational story, an advertiser wants your attention to sell you something. Even most YouTube videos are about generating money for the creator. Realize that only some people want to hear about grandma's garden or the excellent clerk at the supermarket. Probably the most significant "fear" problem is your neighbor or even a stranger calling the police or child protective services if you let your kids play unsupervised – even in your own backyard! Wait a minute – am I creating fear just by writing this? The fear factor is out of control. People who are afraid are much easier to control by those in charge.

The first step to overcoming fear is overcoming your delusions about how scary your neighborhood is. We are suspicious because we haven't taken the time to know our neighbors. I have noticed that in older neighborhoods, every home had a front porch, and people walked, waved to each other, sat and talked, or had morning coffee together. Nowadays we build decks at the back of the house, away from neighbors.

It's time to take the initiative to start a yearly block party with barbecue contests, homemade desserts and games for the kids. Order or make a giant birthday cake and celebrate everyone who has had a birthday during the last year (that's pretty inclusive). Go around the whole group, kids included, and let each share what they are most grateful for this year. You may be shocked at the depth of feelings that come out. Don't wait for someone else to initiate this. Make it your family's adventure and gift to your neighbors.

We should do this!

If you want to live in a safer world, build trust with your neighbors. Don't depend on government people to resolve problems.

As a kid, I remember riding my bike on the subdivision road behind our house. I was riding with my friends when something caused me to fall – probably hit some loose gravel. It knocked me out (nobody wore helmets back then). I remember waking up on a neighbor's kitchen table. The other kids had run for help to this neighbor's house. Nobody called 911 (it hadn't been invented yet), and no ambulance came. No ER exam. After sitting on the table's edge for 5 or 10 minutes, feeling the lump on the side of my head, it was time to ride our bikes again. I don't think anybody even called my parents.

Sure, you are ultimately responsible for the safety of your children, but today's world is different. When you visit a park, museum, or other event, evaluate the overall danger factor. Have a quick discussion with your kids about your observation. Please help them to observe and be alert to their surroundings. Give them some guidelines like staying in sight or hollering distance. Trust the world you are in. When you trust, your kids will relax and enjoy their discoveries all around them. Let their natural curiosities be in control. Someday, they will be totally on their own. Start that confidence-building process even when they are young.

Fear is everywhere because it is a way to easily control you. The whole insurance industry is based on fear. The government wants you living in fear. Even churches - you're going to hell if you don't show up each week and do what I teach you.
You came into this world to experience the beauty and joy of life. It's not a perfect experience, but those rough times often teach us the most.

List some of the fears you have and consider how you can reduce the control of each fear.

Teaching vs. Learning

This is a transition point in the book. We have explored together the different levels of play that kids go through. Hopefully, this has helped you build a better experience for your family. The concept of play is a lifelong game unless it gets stifled. For some reason, most families follow the wide path where we turn our children over to the state at about 5 years old. We allow the state to determine what values should be instilled in these young minds. We let a school put them all in rows on a regimented schedule in a classroom, all the same age.

In the second half of this book, we will explore the concept of "teaching" versus "learning." As we teased at the beginning of this book, growing up doesn't mean giving up play. We just need to move to a more advanced form of play. Utilizing play makes learning fun and more spontaneous. Often times that learning process happens without even realizing it.

Play is the brain's favorite way of learning

~ Diane Ackerman

Diane Ackerman is the author of two dozen highly-acclaimed works of poetry and nonfiction, including New York Times bestsellers The Zookeeper's Wife, A Natural History of the Senses, The Human Age, and Pulitzer Prize Finalist, One Hundred Names for Love.

"I find that writing each book becomes a mystery trip, one filled with mental, emotional (and sometimes physical) adventures. The world revealing itself, human nature revealing itself, is seductive and startling, and that's always been fascinating enough to send words down my spine. But writing a book is only part of the creative process; the circle completes when it settles in a reader's heart. I hope you'll join me on my travels." — Diane Ackerman

You're past the halfway point!

If this book is resonating with you, I also randomly write a newsletter to share ideas with parents and grandparents about how the short time they have with their children can have more depth (and fun). If you would like to read some past issues to see if this appeals to you, go to **www.DiscoveryParkOhio/Blog.htm**

Here are some past titles that might intrigue you:

Touch my Heart
I Love My Cell
My Accidental Job
The Summer Slide
I'm Expecting
Where is Yoda when you need him?
My Feet Wanna Dance
Treasure Maps

Thousands of parents receive these newsletters, and they must be of value since I usually have at least a 40--50% open rate, which I've been told is outstanding.

If you would like to receive these random newsletters, go to https://tinyurl.com/38askjf

We never share or sell this list and you can unsubscribe anytime. I know you're overwhelmed by too many emails already, but this may have value for you.

Thanks, Steve

How We Learn

Let's talk about the Mud Pie Bakery at Discovery Park. It's just a table with some old pans, spoons, and baking tins. Add a bucket of mud and one of water, and let's make something.

It's so fun to watch the magic unfold. Let's put the mud in a mixing bowl, add a little water, mix, and scoop it into a muffin pan. A little sand from the sandbox needs to be sprinkled on top. These pebbles will look good, and a dandelion over there can be picked to go on this muffin.

Some kids, both boys and girls, really get into this experience. They're imitating mom in their own world. They go around and take orders. "The diners wait in anticipation of my wonderful creation." Reality is in the back seat. Imagination is in control.

Maybe they will become chefs or a baker. Maybe their meals will be great for a future family. Maybe they will be a cookie master with a store or sell at a farmers market. They're covered in mud – clothes, hands, and faces. They're loving it. What shall we bake next?

If this is your kid, they're ready to learn how to bake and cook in the real world. Take them in the kitchen and let them discover the magic of real ingredients and ovens. Cooking with mom and dad is incredibly exciting for kids. Perfection isn't important. It's the special time with you that is everything! Keep it fun; they're not in a culinary school.

An experiment was done with young children who supposedly were too young to apply logic to problem solving. The experiment went like this: "All cats bark. Muffin is a cat. Does Muffin bark?" The kids all said NO, cats meow. They are speaking from their real-world experience. However, if the researchers said the same statement in a playful tone, it became clear to the kids that they were talking about a pretend world. Kids as young as four understood the statement's logic and went along with cats barking because they now saw it as a game. Kids at that age are not supposed to be able to use that kind of logic. Even two-year-olds could solve the problem when it was presented as a game.

Similar findings tell us that learning, creativity and problem-solving are very doable through play. The magic is in the playfulness.[7]

Let's focus on one area of learning through play...

READING

Learning how to read is incredibly important. It may be one of the most essential skills to master for a successful life. In our digital culture, the idea of actually reading can be lost or even hidden. With YouTube, TikTok, Netflix, etc...., our world is saturated with visuals. I'm not against that because our brains store info in pictures. If you think back to a special event in your life, images pop up, not a written story about the event.

Reading is a mysterious process. I still remember "See Spot Run" in 2nd grade. "Educators" assume that by building up sentences to be more complex each year, and adding new words through "spelling," you'll someday know how to read. Some learn to read that way, but a shocking number of kids graduate with very limited or no reading skills.

A child can learn to read in 30 hours.[8] It doesn't take years. It's about motivation. When a child decides he wants to understand what all these squiggly lines mean, he can race along from non-reader to proficient reader in a matter of 30 hours spread over one year.[8]

Julie Polanco, a home school mom, questioned that time factor. She has a website called "JulieNaturally". She tried two different reading methods that claimed they could take a non-reader to second-grade level in that time. She used two books: Teach Your Child to Read in 100 Easy Lessons by Siegfried Engelmann and "Delightful Reading" by Lanaya Gore. She stresses that four points need to happen:

1) A stress-free environment

2) Lots of print in the house

3) Wait until the right age

4) Read to them often

"It worked!"

What triggers that exciting journey? You! Your kids want to be just like you. If you are watching TV, playing video games, swiping your phone, etc., that must be what is important. Really?

Let's try an experiment. Grab a fun kids' book. Ask the kids to mentally paint a picture of each page as you read it. Don't let them see what is in the book. After each page (give them plenty of time), ask them to describe their mental picture. Do the next page. When you have reached the end, ask them to retrieve their mental pictures and retell the story. Then, let them see just the words that go with their mental images. Finally, let them see an illustrator's analysis of the words. Don't let them be disappointed in their visual image versus a professional illustrator. Remind them that even the pro started somewhere simpler. The goal is to connect the words with the pictures in their mind. They are not just stand-alone marks to be memorized.

Try reading the story with each of you reading out loud every other word. Put your finger under each word. The goal is their excitement about wanting to know what all those symbols mean. It's like a game. Start with common words like "AND," "TO," and "A." They are trying to remember what each word stands for, like knowing the characters in a story. Individual letters don't mean anything! It's the whole word. Individual letters are like the character having a blue coat. That isn't important. Good readers glance at a word and know it. They know it because they have seen that word thousands of times!

Fantastic readers can read a paragraph with only the first and last letters of each word correct. The letters in the middle can be anything as long as they are the right number of letters for that word. The following example of typoglycemic text was circulated on the Internet in September of 2003: *Aoccdrnig to a rscheearch at Cmabrigde Uinervtisy, it deosn't mttaer in waht oredr the ltteers in a wrod are, the olny iprmoetnt tihng is taht the frist and lsat ltteer be at the rghit pclae.*

Could you read it? **Are you shocked?** If you can't read it, it's because you are reading too slowly and trying to interpret each word. You need to let go of that mind set and let the words flow into your mind. The key is the words are in context, and we seem to "know" what the word is supposed to be.

Back to "teaching" reading, we can't! Kids have to get to the point in their mental development that they want it. If we try to shove it on them when they aren't interested, then resentment toward reading builds up. Now there's an even bigger problem.

In reality, they are surrounded by words – STOP, YIELD, GIANT EAGLE, STARBUCKS, HOBBY LOBBY, etc. They are figuring those signs out without you "teaching" it. When you say you're going to the grocery, they have a mental picture of the building, both inside and out, and they are also visualizing the store sign. As you pick out their favorite foods, the words on the package are recognized. If you showed them a tiny donut and asked them what cereal this was, they would instantly know it was a Cheerio. But their mind would also pull up a picture of the box with the name blazed across it. I used to read many comic books, which helped to increase my reading accuracy and speed.

The most important reading lesson is them seeing YOU loving to read. Do you stop and share a thought that came to you because of what you are reading? Are you saying, "That's a cool idea," "I never thought of it that way," "So that's how it works?" These are all evidence that you are internalizing what you read – it's becoming a part of your life. It's telling your kids that continuing to learn is a lifelong event, and reading is the key to it. **They're listening!**

Play and playful forms of activity potentially lead towards increasingly complex forms of knowledge, skills and understanding

~ Elizabeth Wood

Children learn as they play. Most importantly, in play children learn how to learn

~ O. Fred Donaldson

Do you remember?

Your favorite books?

Story time with a parent/grandparent? Write a few sentences about your memory.

Did you love going to the library? What sections fascinated you the most?

What kinds of books did you like to read?

Are you doing these things with your kids? Story time at the library is not the same as story time with mom or dad! Put them in your lap or snuggle up to them on the couch. That closeness makes a huge difference.

The power of "AH-HA"

There are things in life we never forget. We struggle to understand a problem, and suddenly, the mental light bulb turns on. You've just had an AH-HA moment! Maybe you said it out loud – maybe just to yourself, but it will stick for the rest of your life. It sticks because YOU put the pieces together, you figured it out. You own that discovery.

Someone just telling you the answer isn't the same. You didn't have to work it through – it's their discovery. Chances are you will forget it. That's how it is with much of school. The teacher or book passes on their knowledge. You memorize it for the test and then let it go – you never owned it.

Maybe the above paragraph helped you understand what is happening in your life. Think about what sticks for you. What were your AH-HA moments?

This is how kids learn AND retain best. It's the playful process of discovery. The answers become **your** answers for life.

You have had lightbulb moments! Think about them. Did they change your life's direction? Maybe even the person you married is one of those moments, "This person is awesome, I should marry them!"

Don't rush to the next page. Our goal isn't to get through the book. It's about being renewed by it's insights. Take a few moments and jot down your AH-HA moments.

Is this an "AH-HA" moment?

If you get straight "A's" in school, there is a tendency to think you should be a teacher. So, we have schools full of teachers who believe learning is sharing your knowledge with kids. But it's a struggle if you aren't a great student (good at memorizing). Memorization stinks! **"I'll just try to figure out what the teacher wants to hear so I can get a passing grade."**

But when a real-world job comes, nobody is sitting in rows of desks with the boss lecturing you. You're sitting around a conference table, conferencing – collaborating. It's about a team working together to achieve a big answer. Your A+ doesn't matter. Can you accurately and persuasively share your perspective? Can you critically think it through? Can you develop new approaches that take the game to another level? Can you handle criticism? Does the team value you, not because you're cute or handsome, but because you truly add value?

In today's world, facts can be had with a few keystrokes. The volume of facts and "stuff" is expanding exponentially. Understanding how to work with "stuff" is the real power. Critical thinking, discernment, and common sense are the real skills. Do you know what is propaganda versus truth? Can you see past the BS?

OH MY GOSH

If your kids aren't being taught these skills, it is just entertainment or babysitting.

Developing skills of observation, asking critical questions, and seeing connections to other things will never become obsolete. When kids see you constantly striving to learn, they will understand that learning doesn't stop when you have a diploma in your hand!

Play is not a break from learning.
It is endless, delightful, deep, engaging, practical learning.
It's the doorway into the child's heart

~ Vince Gowmon

IDEAS for creating AH-HA moments:

1 Discover economics by playing Monopoly repeatedly and analyzing different strategies.

2 Use computer simulations to maximize sales at your lemonade stand, run a simulated farm, or create a city.

3 Give them a hundred dollars and ask them how to invest that "financial energy" to increase it, with a deadline of one month to give a report to the board (you).

4 Start a side business with your kids in charge. Let them figure out sales, marketing, production, scheduling, employee management, and bookkeeping.

5 Challenge them to write a song, not just listen to them.

All play is associated with intense thought activity and rapid intellectual growth

~ N. V. Scarfe

The debt we owe to the play of the imagination is incalculable

~ Carl Jung

Play is the beginning of knowledge

~ George Dorsey

The School Corporation

"School is a place where kids learn to be stupid."

~ John Holt, 5th-grade teacher, author, and considered to be one of the founders of the Home School movement

"In 1968, NASA was looking for a way to identify their most creative workers so they would know who to pick out of their large set of employees to tackle the toughest problems. Dr. George Land and Beth Jarman were contracted to create a test that would accurately measure the qualities NASA was looking for. The test calculated the ability of a person to look at a problem and come up with innovative solutions, and it worked remarkably well to help NASA find who they were looking for.

Because the test was so simple, they decided to give it to a group of children who are around the age of five and were representative of the general population of the United States. 98 percent of the children fell into the genius category of imagination.

The five-year-olds were retested at age ten. In just five short years, 68 percent of them had lost their creative-genius status. Another five years went by, and another 18 percent were out of the category. In a span of just one decade, the level of innovative brilliance had dropped by a whopping 86 percent. Then the researchers tested over a million adults with an average age of thirty-one and found that just two percent would match the creative force of almost every five-year-old."[9]

Let me share a familiar story. I was a public school teacher for four years. I loved "teaching" because it was all hands-on in shop classes. We discovered how machines work, how to make a printing plate and run it on a printing press, how to make a drawing in 2D that represented a 3D object. We even learned how to weld metal and cast aluminum. It was all an adventure. Some days, things didn't work. We would discuss what went wrong and try another way the next time. It was like leading a play session every day.

I quit after four years.

1 First, I realized that many of the kids were being sent to my class because it seemed like an easy subject. They weren't old enough to quit school yet without being called truant and getting into trouble with the legal system. These kids had already learned to hate school because they weren't good at taking tests. All their curiosity about life had been sucked out of them. Every class was "boring" because they had already shut down "education". "I'm not good at it."

2 Second, I was fed up with the "system". Since I was a new teacher and didn't hang out in the teacher's lounge, I was assigned lunch monitoring duty every year. Here I am, a skilled teacher, watching kids eat.

3 Third, was all the pressure of constant tests and grading. I didn't care about writing and grading tests. I knew which students were getting it, which ones needed extra guidance and which ones didn't care. How do you test someone on welding? Is his weld better looking than someone else's? What matters was the strength of the weld and there was no way to measure that.

4 Fourth, I realized that schools are corporations with lots of vested interests beyond kids learning stuff. We were all required to be a part of the Union, even if we didn't want to.

The Testing

The tests were to achieve some kind of ranking in the state educational system as if that somehow meant that our teachers were doing a better job than other teachers. Maybe we should have just lied and given every student an A so the rankings would go up. But then we would be investigated for not playing along with the game. At the beginning of each new session, I wanted to announce that if you showed up and tried to discover the joy of working with your hands, you will get an A. I won't even bother with tests. So there - let's have some fun. The administrators were probably glad to see me quit!

I will not allow my education
to be corrupted by my schooling
~ Mark Twain

The opposite of tyrannical evil is play
~ Jordan Peterson

Do not keep children to their studies
by compulsion but by play
~ Plato

This was really hard to write. We have been so accustomed to assuming that going to school was "what one did" when you are a kid. Before I shake your foundations, lets think back to our own school experience. Be honest - this is you talking to you.

GOOD	BAD
______________________	______________________
______________________	______________________
______________________	______________________
______________________	______________________
______________________	______________________
______________________	______________________
______________________	______________________
______________________	______________________
______________________	______________________
______________________	______________________

As you are aware, things change. Schools have changed dramatically! As the Covid experience has shown most parents, the school system is not what it was when you were enrolled.

The next thing I discovered is

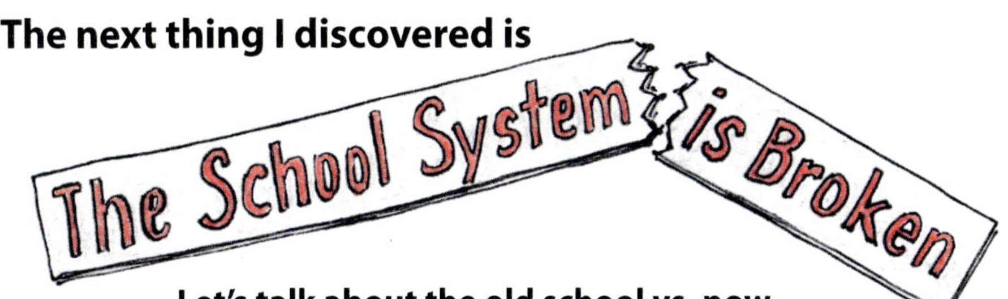

Let's talk about the old school vs. now...

Everybody talks about school reform, but all they want to do is tweak it here and there. The whole system needs to crash. **Many great teachers truly love working with kids and guiding their discovery of the world.** However, many are so frustrated that they are quitting in tears and have no plans for what they will do next week. They are quitting in droves. There is a tremendous teacher shortage, with janitors sometimes called into the classrooms just to meet state regulations.

Yes, some schools are better than others; I get it. People who need to move first ask the realtor, "What are the schools like?". What do you expect them to say, "They're terrible!". They have to tell you what you want to hear because they want to make the sale. Isn't that what life is all about?

The school system was initially set up to train people in basic skills needed in industry. Know how to read a clock and show up for your shift. Read the instructions and follow directions. Don't question authority. In school, there was a system of "units" that you had to achieve before we gave you that magical piece of paper called a diploma. So many units of English, so many units of math and science. We'll toss in a few "you choose" classes to keep you coming, and of course, there was phys. ed. We need strong workers who can lift heavy parts in the factory.

The system has mostly stayed the same. Yes, we now include STEM training and computer programming, but the core units are still there. Consider math classes. I can see classes in trigonometry and algebra for students who intend to go into engineering and science, but most won't. How about a class that simply exposes students to geometry, trigonometry, algebra, coding, basic electricity, hydraulics/pneumatics, and gas engines? Give them just enough understanding so they can grasp the concept.

The same goes for reading. Focus on the different types of books. Teach some storytelling, letter writing, composition skills and more about punctuation.

I've spent forty years in the printing industry, and can assure you that many professionals are terrible spellers who can't compose a good presentation. Thank goodness for spell checkers although I've seen that fail miserably. One lady sent me a text where she offered to give me her kids if I could help her with a project. WHAT? I texted her back to have her look at what she had sent me. We both laughed as she realized her phone was popping up words that she was blindly agreeing to. **Do you proofread your texts and emails?**

Would you like to sit in a hard chair and listen to someone lecture for an hour and be assigned a 1/2 hour's worth of your free time after school as homework? And then there is the next class and the next, all with assignments as if there wasn't enough time in the day to cram it into our heads. It's like an assembly line and as each kid passes by, you dump in your days bit of knowledge. Thank goodness for lunch. Then, back to the classroom!

This is happening at more than just the high school level. Even elementary kids are being assigned homework. (This didn't happen when I was growing up. It takes time for all the day's activities to be absorbed and processed - free time.) Parents are supposed to act as surrogate teachers and sign that their kid did the homework that was assigned. If you complain, you are labeled a troublemaker.

Of course, parents are supposed to tutor their kids if they are having trouble. So now <u>your</u> free time with your family is doing the teacher's job. But wait - there's more. They changed how math is taught, and you have no idea how to help your kid. So your kid is in trouble the next day because you couldn't help them!

This is a book about play. Kids need play in order to assimilate everything they are discovering. **It takes time.** Stress is the opposite of what they need. They need time to work through the skill of reading. If they don't get it when everyone else is getting it, then they are said to have a learning disability. Maybe we'll have to use drugs or put you in special classes "for your kind." Again, as John Holt has proven, it only takes 30 hours to go from non-reader to proficient reader. It's just about opening that door when they are ready to go through it. Opening the door early and pushing them through it will only lead to resentment. You are killing their spirit. The same goes with math and every other "subject."

Here are some ideas for you.

Reading: Find a really goofy, laugh-out-loud book. Read it together. If you have a slow reader, have them put their finger on the page. Let it follow the words. This helps the eye stay focused (eyes are still developing) and can increase reading speed by up to 20%. Also, snuggle up with them on the couch. They need that contact with you to settle into the adventure.

If a fun story has different characters, let different kids read each character's part. Encourage them to "play" the part so they aren't so focused on their reading but are focused on vocal style (speed, intonation, vocal range, etc.). This will help them let go of embarrassment if they are a slow reader. They can make up for it by their character development. They are discovering that reading is a fun adventure.

Math: Learn to make change. Put prices on some empty food packages and practice adding different items up. Eventually, see how close you can come by adding the item's prices in your head. Give them a $20 bill and challenge them to get the most for that bill. Then, talk about nutritional choices and let them choose again.

How many books do your kids have? Pick ten. Count how many words are on a page. Estimate how many words are in a book? Do this for each book – add them up and divide by 10 (books) to see the average number of words (or pages) in a book.

Chemistry:

1. Make cookies.
2. Use the same recipe, but vary the amount of each ingredient to see how it affects the taste.
3. Vary the baking time and temperature. Do very small batches. This will also use math to convert the amounts.

This could even be shown in graphs.

Physics:

1. Go to a playground and measure the angle of a slide.
2. Time how long it takes to go down.
3. Wax the slide and re-test the speed.

Advanced students could also calculate the average speed if they measured the length of the slide.

How high (angle) can a swing go? Why not higher? What is the cycle time from high point to high point and back? How does the length of the swing chains affect these numbers?

Kids want to experience life, not hear a teacher explain it, read about life, or see it on a screen. They want to be immersed in the adventure, not told to wait for the slowest kid to finish or that there will be a test tomorrow.

When the field trip buses pull up at Discovery Park Ohio, the kids are practically crawling out the windows. They can't wait for today's discoveries. Many leaders have told me that this place is their most anticipated field trip of the summer.

I love questions. They are door openers. When I talk to parents at our park, I usually ask them something about their work. It seems innocent and common. But then I start going deeper. What challenges does their work have? Is it fun? What would they change?

Tell me about your job:

____

____

____

____

Learning happens all the time. We can't stop it. Every interaction will affect each child's view of the world they are living in.

I want to share some insights from award-winning retired teacher John Taylor Gotto. I believe these points were in a YouTube video.

John spent much of his life teaching 8th grade in New York City and was awarded teacher of the year both locally and state-wide several times. He points out that **school is easy**, because someone else tells you what to do and how to do it. Unfortunately, that leads to kids becoming dumber because their natural curiosity is being crowded out by a day full of standing in line, waiting, sitting at a desk, waiting, doing whatever you are told to do, waiting, and even homework which cuts into your "free" time to explore your world on your terms. In addition, the curriculum is determined by someone else – not you.

Education, however, is hard. It is self-initiated and requires you to take charge of your own life. So, John brings up the huge differences between what the public schools and even many homeschoolers teach versus what the "elite, rich" parents want for their child's education.

The wealthy send their kids to about 20 premier schools. Often, those teachers don't even have teaching certificates. Of course, their kids need to learn basics, and they know that each of those subjects (reading, math, etc.) can easily be taught in 30 to 50 hours total time. It's the timing. When does the child have the drive to go for it? When they are totally fascinated by a book, they will figure out how to read it quite quickly, and then there is no stopping them.

Mr. Gotto shares some things the elite want their kids to learn that aren't found in most schools. You can do this too. It doesn't take a lot of money.

1 **Manners/Etiquette.** A child who is always polite, knows how to treat others, and does it automatically to EVERYONE will be welcomed everywhere. (I see this every day at Discovery Park. Some kids automatically help others get the train back on the track, taking turns, encouraging each other, and giving a helpful push on the go-karts. It's not just their family they are being polite to; it's everyone else in the park. Even as they leave, they thank me for all the fun, without their parent's reminder.)

2 **Hard intellectual knowledge** – not watered down/simplified. They want their kids to work at understanding complex relationships and ideas. Read Moby Dick together and see the difficulty of managing a crew on a dangerous voyage to catch an elusive whale. It's not about the whale. Get the original text, not some sissified version that simplifies everything. D. H. Lawrence called it "one of the strangest and most wonderful books in the world."

3 **The advice given** to their children should be from people the parents know, trust, and respect. There are too many agendas that can easily distort your child's life. Get to know those interacting with your children – teacher, guidance counselor, coach. Invite them to dinner or a cookout or meet them at a restaurant. They will probably be shocked at your passion to know your kids' influencers.

4 **Inspire a love** and appreciation of the land, animals, and the natural world. It will always surround us, sustain us, and bring our hearts back in tune.

5 Their kids should learn **a public sense of decorum** (behavior with good taste and propriety). They should be able to adapt naturally to every situation with knowledge and sympathy.

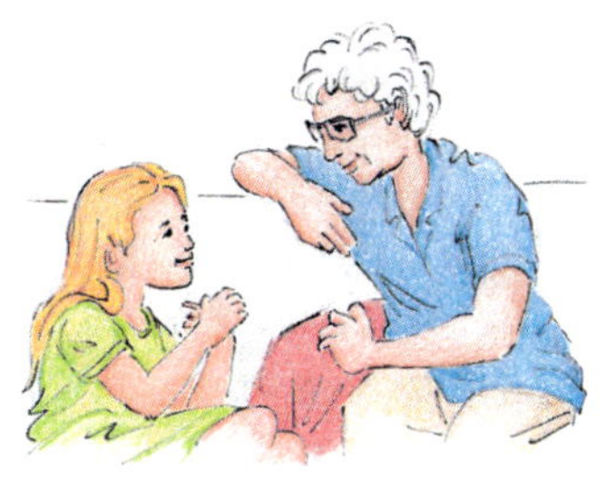

6 They need a **common core of shared ideas/values.** Can they easily speak with Grandma because we value the same basic things?

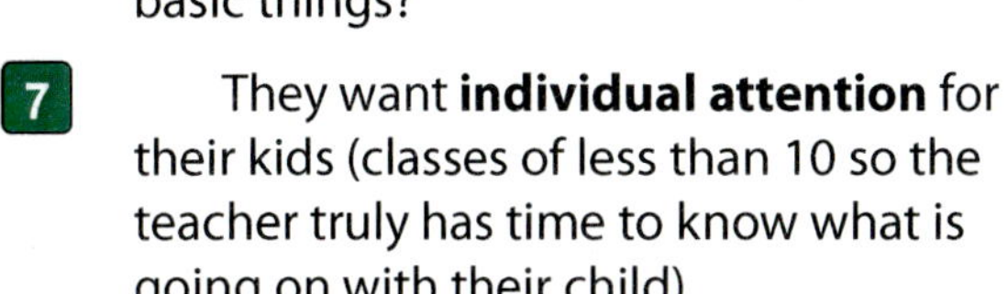

7 They want **individual attention** for their kids (classes of less than 10 so the teacher truly has time to know what is going on with their child).

8 **Push kids in their interests.** Kids become fascinated by different "things". Give them time to explore in depth. Push them to see all the connections the "thing" has to other "things." Challenge them to push beyond their internal boundaries. Never let them be satisfied with just an OK performance.

9 They must **learn to write well.** Start a journal. Every evening, write what you "discovered" that day. Not a list of what you did. Push deeper. What profound statement did Grandma make? Am I satisfied with my own growth today? What impacted me at dinner? Start with a minimum of 300 words (about 30 sentences).

10 **Leadership exercises** – they do not want their kids to have a managed/manipulated herd mentality. Their kids must know how to rise above the crowd and think/decide for themselves. This involves public speaking, critical thinking, and the ability to debate.

11 **Accuracy in observation.** Try drawing something or describing something. Did you get the proportions right? How about the lighting and the shadows? Were there details you glossed over? Accurately observing your environment, people, the feeling and the mood will sharpen every skill you are developing.

12 Never go to a book if you can **talk to the author.**

I read a book about gardening that was way beyond any other gardening book I had ever read. The author, I discovered, lived in Norwalk, Ohio, just an hour away. I contacted him, we had dinner together, and he showed me stuff that was way beyond what was even in his book. We became lifelong friends.

All of these ideas are relatively inexpensive. But you do need to invest time in your kids. Each skill you work at with them is also a skill you are learning. When YOU start a journal, soon your kids will want their own journal. Your kids need to see you writing and wanting to grow wiser, not just older. Pick one, and go for it!

Play is training for the unexpected

~ Marc Bekoff

Here are some truths the Ivy League Universities probably don't want you to know.

1) You may get the best education - that doesn't guarantee a wow job. That job category may not even exist by the time you graduate.

2) Most Ivy Leagues have so much money in the bank from endowments, that most students could go for free.

3) Their statistics about how few are accepted is skewed. They market their school heavily so thousands of young people apply so the few that are accepted feel very special.

4) Many times it isn't the knowledge you are receiving, but the connections you are building with other wealthy and influential people.

But hey, focus on the 12 steps above and skip the money game.

Most Teaching is Worthless!

What do you remember from your early years? I'm betting that very few memories come from the classroom teacher. When a teacher tells us something, we have to remember that item. We probably didn't want to remember that bit of info, but we knew there would be a test. Then we could forget it. Remember spelling tests?

Knowledge that stays with you isn't done to please the teacher or parent. **Real learning comes from our discoveries about life**. As I shared earlier, I call them AH-HA moments! I put it together, so now I own it. It is my discovery!

Play is actually the most effective learning mode. As we play, we are figuring things out and trying new approaches. What works and what doesn't? Great teachers at school or home understand this, They don't give answers; **they create situations that allow students to discover answers**. How they figure it out isn't essential, and rewarding them with a star or a grade isn't essential. It's the discovery. Even working as a team to come up with the answers works because those who aren't getting it see how everyone else is working through the assignment, and as peers, they aren't afraid to admit they don't get it. Usually someone on the team can explain it at the same level they are at. This even works for mixed-age groups.

But today's schools are consumed with testing. Currently, students take about 150 tests between the time they enter the school system and the time they graduate. These aren't spelling tests. These are major assessment tests. That works out to about one big test every 15 days! There isn't time to explore; we have to memorize for the next test. The schools' aim is to show the world how great we are as educators.

I talked with a local retired superintendent of schools. He stopped at the local gas station and bought some snacks. At that time, you had to figure out the change for the customer. He recognized the young man behind the counter had just graduated from his school. The kid couldn't figure out the proper change. The superintendent went home very depressed.

The school system is failing kids on every front. Every year, we graduate more and more students who are terrible readers and can only do simple math. They don't understand money, interest rates, the credit system, and money management. They don't understand geography and can't point out where the United States is on the globe. There are cringe-worthy videos on YouTube asking basic questions that any student should know about the world by the time they leave High School. The students being asked are usually college students. You'll shake your head in disbelief. How did they get out of High School, and how did they ever get accepted into college.

What if we turn all these weaknesses into games and play mode? Then they can learn these life-affirming skills.

Here's a good example: Does anyone remember the early computer game called "Where in the world is Carmen Sandiego?"

The original (1985) "Where in the World Is Carmen Sandiego?" video game was classified as a "mystery exploration" series by creators and the media. The series would later be deemed edutainment when the games became unexpectedly popular in classrooms. The franchise centers around the fictional thieving villain of the same name, the ringleader of the criminal organization V.I.L.E. The protagonists (most often including the in-game character controlled by the computer user) are agents of the ACME Detective Agency who try to thwart the crooks' plans to steal treasures from around the world, while the ultimate goal is to capture Carmen Sandiego herself.

The franchise primarily focuses on teaching children geography, but has also branched out into history, mathematics, language arts, and other subjects.

BLURRED VISION

Following trends may lead to blindness. I know that's a crazy statement. I'm not referring to social or political trends.

We spend so much time now staring at electronic screens. Many kids have a laptop on their desk at school. We use computers and other screens almost constantly in our lives. Even many jobs have you sitting in front of a screen all day.

Eye doctors are reporting that the number of kids suffering from severe myopia or nearsightedness (blurriness at a distance) is skyrocketing. Even though they could see the trend over the last 15 years, the "why" was elusive. After extensive testing, they found that it wasn't genetics. Finally, the head of optometry research at Ohio State University figured it out. There is too much extended close-up looking and poor lighting.

In Japan and China, the myopia pandemic has been particularly hard hit (80%). Japan and China put a heavy emphasis on studying to get ahead. Kids were always reading, working on problems, and studying. All that close-eye work was causing eye damage. Now Asian schools require mandatory recess time to give the eyes a break. American kids are at 50% and growing.

How does this relate to play? When schools eliminated much of the playground time, this also aggravated eye problems. Playground time allows the eyes to focus on distant objects. Although kids can see at an early age, their eyes continue to grow and develop as the rest of their body grows.

Suppose they are constantly looking at their world close up. In that case, their eyes gradually adapt to this and can no longer adjust properly to distance viewing.

The same research showed that a much higher light level (preferably Natural light) needs to be maintained. Also kids should be outdoors at least two hours a day to focus on distant objects. This is especially tough during the winter. Kids leave for school early and arrive home as the sun is setting.

Here are my thoughts:

1 When reading or doing other activities that require heavy eye usage (computer games), make sure the kids are at least **18 inches away** from books, paperwork, or screens. This is longer than most of their arms, so it is challenging. If they can't read clearly at that distance, it's time for an eye checkup. Also, when you are hunched over to read – books or screens – it impacts your posture which can lead to other health problems.

2 Teach your kids to **look up every few minutes** and focus on something farther away. This will give your eyes a well-needed rest. Tiny muscles around the eye lens allow the eye to focus on objects at different distances. Hold your arm out in front of you. It won't be long before your arm needs a rest. Different muscles take turns holding up your arm, but eventually, they all get tired and need a break. The same is happening with your eyes.

3 **Increase the brightness** and quality of the light. Teach your kids how to make the light come over their shoulder so it doesn't glare off the surface into their eyes. Use full spectrum lighting if possible. Keep it bright, but don't have a dark background. The strong contrast is also hard on the eyes.

4 **Spend time outdoors**, even in the winter. Research shows kids (and you, too) must be outdoors at least two hours a day. Bundle up – you can do it! Look up the website 1000 hours outside. "Ginny," the author, has many great ideas for outdoor fun, even in winter.

5 **Your eyes need sunlight!** Unless you are being blinded by the glare of the snow, try to avoid sunglasses. "But they make me look cool, mysterious." Eyes need the natural rays of the sun. I'm not talking about looking directly at the sun but letting the sun's energy bounce off objects and into your eyes. Sunglasses and auto-tinting glasses defeat that. I haven't used sunglasses in years, and I'm outdoors almost daily, especially in the summer. Yes it's bright, but my eyes can handle it.

I'm going to make a big jump here. Just a thought. If you are always looking at a screen – a small piece of reality, can you step back far enough to see the big picture? In so many ways, we see the little problems all around us. But can we step back to see the bigger picture of what's happening with your family relationships, town, country, and world?

TO SCHOOL - OR NOT TO SCHOOL

A good playground invites discovery. So does a walk in the fields or woods. Imagine a trip to a working farm, feeding animals and sitting in the cab of a big tractor or combine. Most kids will love these adventures. Go on factory tours and smell up a bakery. They will spend the whole day with more questions than you thought possible. What is happening? They are self-educating! The entire world is waiting to be discovered!

Kids are learning all the time. Just because they aren't in a classroom doesn't mean they shut their minds off. Kids of every age learn best by trying ideas to see if they work. If they don't, they try something else (just like a scientist). This learning process leads to permanent knowledge because it is their discovery.

When we teach and announce they will be tested on it, students play the game of remembering the answer just long enough for the test. **Actually, telling (teaching) kids stunts the learning process.** Has your kid ever said "I can do it myself!"? Pick up on that! They are telling you they want to figure it out for themselves.

Remember what John Holt, long-time 5th-grade teacher and the godfather of the homeschooling movement, said, "School is a place where kids learn to be stupid." He is saying the system forces kids into a learning path that is pretty rigid and usually to the level of the slowest in the room. Please know that there are some excellent teachers who get it. But they are working in a system that undermines many of their skills.

Kids naturally love to learn. Today, they want to know everything about frogs. Where do they live, what do they eat, can they bite, and are they slippery? To satisfy this intense curiosity may take a day or a week. Do you really want to stop inquisitiveness, that enthusiasm and say "it's time for arithmetic"?

Play is the most powerful learning technique. I seldom answer their questions as I watch and interact with the kids and parents at Discovery Park. I give them hints and suggestions and open new ideas.

I am blatantly biased about how kids learn.

If your kids hate going to school, get them out! You want them to love life and love to learn. If that isn't being fostered in your school - for your child - then it's time for a change. Yes, public schools are free (taxes), but there are also Montessori and Waldorf schools, homeschooling, micro-schools, and even a concept called "un-schooling".

You chose to bring these children into the world. Don't turn them over to a stranger who will instill their values into them. If they learn to just do as they're told and follow directions, they

may spend the rest of their lives on an assembly line or sitting in a cubicle. They need to know how to figure things out on their own, spot propaganda and lies, work with money, build solid friendships, and live independently and not in your basement. How are they going to learn these essential, lifelong skills?

Now I have to admit that not every kid is going into adulthood as a genius. Finding what fits you is the most important part. Maybe you like the idea of an assembly line. You know you are creating something the world values or shipping a product so it gets there on time. Your life is consistent, predictable. That gives you the freedom to step out in your private life. You can participate in the community theater or you rule a certain video game. I get it, we're all wired differently.

This week, I spoke to a retired father who was very concerned about our educational system. I asked him what woke him up to this issue. He said, "I saw a crossing guard guiding High School students across the street."

The change is never going to start at the top. **YOU have to take control** of the situation. You love your kids. Every kid learns differently – at a different pace. You know it, you can see it. Schools can't adapt to your child's learning style.

It may seem overwhelming to consider Home Schooling or an alternative school, but at least focus on play - the most effective way to learn.

The true object of all human life is play

~ G. K. Chesterton

When children pretend, they're using their imaginations to move beyond the bounds of reality. A stick can be a magic wand. A sock can be a puppet. A small child can be a superhero

~ Fred Rogers

Necessity may be the mother of invention, but play is certainly the father

~ Roger Von Oech

So tell yourself what direction each of your kids seem to be going. Write it down now, so when you look back, yo can see if you observed (or guessed) well.

Alternatives to Public School

Although this is a book about play, the role that schools play in the children's lives is immense. Kids need to figure out many skills to become happy and successful in life, and how they achieve that goal varies greatly.

The public school system has an enrollment of about 49.4 million students. Private schools have about 5.5 million, and Home Schools account for about 3.7 million students as of 2023. Private schools include religious schools, Montessori Schools, Waldorf Schools, micro-schools and many other types. Preschools are not included in these numbers. Many of these alternative schools use play-based learning. For those unfamiliar with alternative systems, here is a very brief intro so you can explore your options more fully.

Religious schools teach in ways similar to public schools but add in religion classes. So this type of school is not different in character from public schools other than the moral teachings and a better discipline system.

Montessori Schools

Montessori schools are mixed-age classrooms and no grades or homework. At Montessori schools, younger children have long blocks of time—up to three hours at once—to freely interact with specially developed learning materials. As children get older, they participate in extensive research

projects, which they present to their class. At all ages, you won't see rows of desks or assigned seats. Students are welcome to move about classrooms to freely choose what to work on.

Waldorf Schools

Waldorf schools are based on the philosophy of education that children learn, grow, and develop best when you tend to all aspects of their beings – not just the academic ones.

In a Waldorf school, you won't see kids sitting all day at their desks, listening to the teacher standing in the front of the room. Instead, kids learn through art, play, cooking, music, and outside exploration.

Kids spend a lot of time outdoors, in almost all weather (bundled up, in winter).

Screens are not used in the classroom and are discouraged outside of the school as well.

There is an emphasis on loving and respecting nature. Many art activities use natural materials from nature such as leaves and beeswax.

Teachers use music and storytelling to deliver many of their lessons.

Children participate in cooking, cleaning, knitting, and jewelry making.

Movement and play are emphasized in the early grades as the primary way of learning.

Micro schools are also growing. Perhaps the fastest-growing one is the Acton Academy which originated in Austin, Texas, in 2009. This system uses guides who do not teach, but prompt students through discovery processes utilizing questions. The kids run the school and even self-discipline. It is a mixed-age group with approximately 30 students or less in a studio. The number of schools is growing exponentially, with over 300 schools around the world. Academically, the kids are way ahead of their peers in the public system.

Home Schooling

Home schools have a vast array of teaching styles. First, the children are not going to another building/teacher to learn. They are being taught by one or both parents. Most parents choose special courses (curriculum) developed especially for the home school community. Some are very rigid with specific classes, while some are very loose, giving the parent simple guidance on things they may want to include. Some may use computers and most make sure their kids visit many museums and field trips to broaden their learning. Also, many belong to home-school groups that gather regularly so their kids can intermingle with other kids in the movement.

Although John Holt is seen as the father of home schooling back in the 1980s, his real understanding of how kids learn led him to believe that the best way for kids to learn was through their own initiative. The parent acts as an advisor and guidance person. He strongly believed that kids will become well-balanced in all areas given the space and time to pursue their interests. He called this **un-schooling**. Unfortunately, many parents are afraid that their kids won't end up with a balanced education on their own and feel that they, as parents, have a duty to "teach" key concepts.

The beauty of homeschooling is that the parent knows exactly where their children are in their development, and most days, they can complete all their assignments in just a few hours, leaving much of the day for free play (where much of the real learning is happening).

The home schooling movement is growing rapidly, especially after parents saw what their kids were exposed to through video teaching during the pandemic.

The real question of all types of schooling is, "Which is better training for life?". This goes back to the question of how kids learn through play. Real life is an informal game. The rules can change at any moment, and you participate in that process. There are no specific winners or losers. Getting along with others is far more important than beating someone - even if they are the competitor. Someday, the companies may merge, or you may switch jobs and now work for that competitor. What matters is how you play the game, how much fun you have along the way and the joy you are giving others. This is not just about work, but about all life. And these are the skills kids learn as they play. Will you ever need to know how to throw a perfect curve ball or shoot a free throw? The real skills are the negotiating skills learned on the playground, because everyone wants the game to keep going.

Play is the work of the child

~ Maria Montessori

Almost all creativity involves purposeful play

~ Abraham Maslow

On Being the Parent/Adult

Let's challenge ourselves to start seeing children in a new way. Most of our notions of child care and education are founded on agricultural metaphors of the 1800s, the agricultural era, was when the concept of the state educating a child took hold. We raise children, like a garden or chickens. We train children, like training a horse, so he does what we command him to do. Our attitude has been one of ownership: we brought you into this world from that initial seed and therefore, we own you, and we will tell you how to

behave and, what you are going to learn, and even what we believe you should be when you become an adult. If your parents treated you that way, then I'm sure there is some resentment lurking inside. Do I only get to live the life I really want after you die, or are your directives even written in your will?[10]

We are all born with a spirit that also guides our growth. It doesn't force us into a paticular path because there is always free will. Spirit knows that many lessons are learned from challenging experiences and mistakes. If a child is allowed to feel/listen to that inner voice, they will move smoothly through life. It doesn't mean it will be bump-free; he just knows that he has the right and ability to choose the life he wants. That may change - often. We learn from every experience, and what we thought we wanted one day may not be what we need tomorrow. Even relationships are like that. Everyone wants to date the head cheerleader or the football star, but the girl on the playground who is always teasing you or catching you in a game of tag may be the one you are supposed to be with.

Being a trustful parent will allow your child to bloom. You let your kids play and explore on their own, to make their own decisions, take risks and learn from their mistakes. Trustful parents aren't neglectful. They provide sustenance, love, guidance, respect, moral examples and an environment that is required for healthy development. They are supportive rather than directive as the child grows. They help the child achieve the goals - when asked for.

I admit, I loved writing this. I'm old, but young. I've had wonderful experiences and tragedies. Through it all, I knew I was supposed to go through this to learn how to love more deeply. Whether we have arrived at that understanding or not, we are all spiritual beings. This temporary vessel we call a body can stop at any time. But our spirit does not die. If you have not heard of this concept, search out videos on Near Death Experiences (NDE). The stories they will share will uplift your heart.

Learning to live a life of gratitude will change your attitude. My last wife had MS. She home schooled my kids as best she could. Now my daughter has a daughter who has a genetic anomaly that keeps here from being anything close to normal. But my daughter loves that girl. So inspiring. The key to that attitude is gratitude. Life isn't perfect, but our attitude changes our perspective.

I am grateful for: ______________________________

____

____

____

____

Emotional Distress

"The decline of children's free play since about 1955 has been accompanied by a continuous rise in anxiety, depression, and feelings of helplessness in young people. Related to these findings, there has been an increase in **narcissism** and a decline in **empathy**."[11]

These two terms are directly related. Narcissism is an inflated view of self, which tends to separate the self from others and prevent the formation of meaningful two-way relationships. In a relatively direct relationship, the decline in empathy involves not caring about other people.

When kids are kept from normal playful interactions at an early age, the ability to define themselves in a realistic way and care about their playmates is crushing. Allowing children to have plenty of time for free play is crucial to the healthy development of relationship skills. With the recent pandemic lockdowns, many teachers report that even at the preschool and early elementary ages, many of these kids are truly struggling with properly interacting, with much more lashing out at the smallest provocation.

Also, the role of mask-wearing eliminated their ability to understand subtle facial clues. I know you are just lightly teasing by the smile on your face kind of thing. This is especially important because we know that more than 65% of our communication is non-verbal, as in reading the other person's body language. If I'm not around other kids to learn these subtle clues, I may misinterpret the motives behind what they say.

Off the record

There are far more boys who are labeled ADHD than girls. Why?

I visit about 60 pre-schools every year. I've only seen two male teachers. Most elementary schools have female teachers. Many of their classrooms have a distinctive feminine feel to them. Of course, that's their personality coming through. But the energy levels and values of boys are completely different from girls. They want to run, wrestle, jump and challenge. It's hormonal. All that energy rushing through their body is struggling to get out. They can't sit still. They get bored easily. They don't see the point of a certain lesson. Another coloring page - really? So they get sent to the office, and passed down through the specialists. Let's just medicate him.

I'll leave it at that.

So have you experienced this or are dealing with it?

Spoken from the Heart

Think about it... We have explored how play is such a great way to learn. We've had those AH-HA moments. **I want to go to the next level.**

There are experiences we have or will have that deeply move us. A child watching a baby chick being born is one of those incredible moments. They will remember that wonder for the rest of their life.

Let me share a story that has moved me deeply.

> "A man dies in an accident and is an organ donor. His heart is placed in another man who desperately needs a transplant. The first man's wife is now widowed.
>
> After several years, the widow finds out who got her husband's heart and sets up a time to meet him and see how his heart has worked out in his life. He tells her that it completely changed his life – to the point that his wife divorced him, claiming he was no longer the man she had fallen in love with. That was hard, and confusing.
>
> As they talked, the widow felt a connection to the divorced man. He seemed to have many of the same values and characteristics as her deceased husband. They continued to get to know each other, fell in love, and eventually married."

Interesting!

We are usually taught that the brain is where thinking happens. We analyze, evaluate, remember, and make decisions in our heads. I'm not so sure. There are so many phrases that we use that imply the heart is where decisions come from.

Consider the following phrases:

- What does your heart say?
- A heartfelt thanks
- Follow your heart
- Speak from the heart
- Having a heavy heart
- Your heart needs mending

Perhaps the brain is more like a hard drive where we keep memories, procedures, patterns, and calculation techniques. The brain can run the body, do the job, and get you to the right place. But I believe the heart finds the joy, love and passion in our lives. Yes, the mind can drive the body, but the heart creates the spark that is you.

Let's take that idea to the next level. Life is about interacting with people – kids, spouses, parents, siblings, bosses, co-workers. As you interact, start refining those events into heart connections, not brain connections. Don't analyze the situation. Let your heart guide you. That is easy with some interactions but hard with others. But when you speak to someone with gentleness, kindness, genuine concern – that's heart talk.

When you listen, be active, trying to understand why they are saying that and what they are really driving at. Don't think about what you are going to say or a rebuttal. Take a deep breath – ponder – give a slow, thoughtful response. It will change the dynamics of every interaction.

Life is about learning how to love more deeply. Learning to love those that don't seem loveable is the real challenge – and success.

Pour your heart out (not your brain)! It will get stepped on as others fumble around in life. The risk is worth it. You will survive and keep growing.

Don't Talk Back!

Teachers say it, I've said it, you've probably said it. There are times when **kids are just plain annoying**. Why – Why – Why? Stop a minute and analyze what is really going on.

Maybe these antics, these "games," aren't meant to drive you crazy but are really pleas for your attention.

Maybe the "talking back" is because you haven't seen their perspective. It's easy to say, "Because I told you so." Did that really help the situation? That was just frustration talking.

Put your hand up to signal "STOP". Take a deep breath and a pause. Ask your kids what they really need, want, or disagree with. Listening isn't giving in. It's caring. Maybe they need your attention. They don't have a reason, they want YOU. Perhaps they need a hug, a sit and talk time or milk and cookies. Really listening can diffuse almost every tense moment, even with a spouse or co-worker, ... or a teenager!

This is a test of your heart talk.

The playing adult steps sideward into another reality;
the playing child advances forward to new stages of mastery

~ Erik H. Erikson

I'm guessing , that if you, "the reader," are female, that you rarely talked back. That was your brother's calling. He was always getting into trouble.

Whether you're female (you were sooo feisty) or male, you had some "talking back" events. Write them down. What do you think was really going on?

___

___

___

___

___

___

___

___

___

___

___

___

Do You EMOTE?

Kids emote! They don't realize it. They just do. Emoting is typically considered an **exaggerated display of emotion**. It is most commonly seen in the theatrical sense. Adults rarely emote unless angry or caught up in a heated debate. After years of being told to sit down, be quiet, etc., we have given up being expressive.

"Hello, how are you?" "I'm fine." Worthless words – platitudes – empty of feeling. Wouldn't it be more fun to answer, "It's another beautiful day to be alive!" or "I can't wait to see what today's adventures will bring!"

Answers like these start connections and interactions. They catch the other person completely off-guard. They want to interact, to "catch" what you have. Even a negative answer like "I'm having a rough morning" can create a positive interaction. The key is – you're being honest. Honesty surprises others.

If you have ever studied "non-verbal communication", you know that only about 35% of communication occurs through words. The other 65% comes through our body language, vocal inflection, and facial expressions.

When you are around someone who understands how to communicate with their whole body, you are invariably intrigued. Flailing arms don't count. Their face is expressive. Their voice has variability and pauses. They are talking <u>to you</u>, not looking around or at the phone. Your eyes meet, smiles break out, or maybe a frown. You are connected. You want to keep the conversation going. You want to know this person.

Imagine reading a story to kids. "Once upon a time.. " You can just read it like any other sentence, or you can generate mystery, excitement, and desire if you put your whole heart into the phrase. The phrase can be said whimsically, with curiosity, boldly, or as a matter of fact. Each way you say it draws in the audience to the rest of the story differently.

Likewise, learning to let your "emotions," your "heart and soul," come out in your words will dramatically change the dynamics of your relationships. Consider the phrase "I love you". Add one word – "I really love you" and it changes everything. Your heart is now talking instead of just your brain.

Most people desperately want/need approval. You could say, "Nice job", but why not say, "I really like the way you did.... " has approval written all over it.

Straighten up, walk tall, smile, uncross your arms, lean into a conversation. Learn to emote. It shouldn't be theatrical, but work on letting your feelings and your heart come into your conversations. Your heart's truthfulness may open some surprising doors.

And your kids will genuinely note the difference. See if the way they are interacting starts changing, too.

Trying to define play is like trying to define love. You can't do it. It's far too big for that

~ Gordon Sturrock

Story Reader or Story Teller?

We have all experienced the joy of reading a story to our kids, usually after dinner or at bedtime. The world of colorful books available for kids is a treasure trove waiting to be explored. . If you're not yet reading to your kids (even the older ones), you're missing out on a delightful family bonding event. Reading to your kids should be a regular, even daily, occurrence, and it's an activity that should involve not just Mom or Dad, but also older siblings.

Let us go past the words on the page. Unless you are a swift wit, consider reading the book without the kids first. Take time to feel the author's theme, their rhythm, and mood. Is this story comical, serious, moody, dramatic, or inquisitive? You've just taken your first step to becoming a storyteller. **The most significant difference between being a reader and a storyteller comes from inside you.**

A story reader uses the brain to read words, but a storyteller uses the heart to immerse the listener **in** the story. Each character in the story should have their own unique voice, speed and even rhythm. Theses voices can be tough, soft, sweet or matter-of-fact. By reading the book first, you can build a sense of character beyond the words. Think about how each sentence can gain more depth because you've taken the time to feel the words.

Most children's books rely way too much on the pictures. Without the pretty pictures, the story wouldn't even be worth reading. So, pick books that have meaningful depth. These are the ones you should spend time with. A good story is painting a picture in the listener's mind. It becomes their story because we will each paint a little different picture.

So now it's time to be the "Storyteller". Don't let them see the pictures. Paint the images with the sounds of your voice, body language, and the look on your face. Don't be timid. Mentally, be on your stage, performing for the most important people in your world. As you hone your confidence (that is probably more important than skill), look for ways to draw your audience into the story. Maybe there is a line that keeps repeating. Get them to say it with you.

There are books about how to be a great "storyteller," but this is just you and the family.

When relatives or friends come over, ask them if they have a favorite story from their past to share. Did they have a dog, cat, raccoon or squirrel as a pet? Was there an event that went totally wrong or unexpected? Before long, everyone will be remembering those crazy times, important moments, moving events that make life so interesting. You've started a storytelling frenzy, and in the process, you're creating a space for everyone to share their personal stories and connect on a deeper level.

Storytelling helps you become a real person to your kids, not just the angry parent who demands they clean their room or the maid, chef, and chauffeur. When kids realize you are a real person who's done stupid things, laughed till the milk came out of your nose, or even failed but have learned from that failure, that's when a family bonds!

I really want to be a storyteller. It's on my list. All of history was passed on by storytelling. Gathered around the fire, relating an historical event, a creepy, scary story, looking at the stars and talking about the trip you're going to take to mars. Or maybe it's one of the funniest moments of your life. Tell the story.

Stop and write down some ideas:

Floating Through Life

Do you remember what you had for dinner two nights ago? Do you remember what you did last Friday night? Life is slipping by, often out of our grasp. We lived it, but have we captured it? Maybe it wasn't worth capturing, but that's another story.

How about starting a new passion? Try to capture the moments of your life before they flee away. Grab a pen, and let's go after them. As the day winds down, a quiet time helps your body slow down and prepare for sleep. **Turn off the mindless screens and take the time to reflect on your day.** Start a journal. Grab a booklet that has no lines. Don't use a computer. Your eyes need a rest from screens.

You will need two writing instruments, a good ballpoint pen and an old-fashioned pencil or a drawing pencil. You probably don't even own a pencil sharpener anymore, so grab a simple, pocket-size sharpener. The ballpoint is essential because the ink won't run or smear if your paper gets wet. Here we go...

Print, it's faster than script. Write whatever is flowing into your mind. Don't worry about the organization, spelling or punctuation. You are capturing your thoughts. In the quiet stillness before bed, start thinking about the day. The schedule doesn't matter. We are not making a list of what happened. We will reflect on what moved us, the funny things we all laughed at, and what made us sad or angry. What insights happened? Did my child do something profound or disturbing? Why do I think that happened? How did it change my expectations, understanding, or direction?

We're pushing ourselves deeper to explore how life is moving us, how subtle changes in my family are developing. How am I changing and reacting? What interaction did I have with my partner? Did it help us grow closer or farther? This is where you can start actually seeing the story of your life unfold. Don't spend much time looking back at what you already wrote, focus on the now. Write down those emotions - put them in your journal, so you don't have to carry them around in your head.

"Can't I just use the pictures on my phone as a life journal?" Does your phone reflect your thoughts and feelings? Pictures on your phone help, but it is not a substitute for an actual journal. Stopping long enough to write your thoughts helps you to examine your life and where it is going.

Don't force yourself to write every day, especially if you're exhausted. This is to help you stay focused, not become another chore. Your head needs a fresh slate each day, not a basket of burdens from previous days. Writing today's journey down helps you let go and start fresh the next day.

"What about the pencil?" Sometimes words don't work. Try sketching. It may feel awkward or silly at first, but as you sketch more and more, it will force you to really look at the world. That's the real goal. We look but don't see. When you sketch, you really have to look. How many petals does that flower have? How are they arranged with each other? Are they identical or varying? What you sketch doesn't matter. Maybe it's a landscape or the look on your child's face. Maybe you're drawing from your imagination.

This is your treasure box to store the important memories and dreams of what you want to see. Write down your goals, short and long-term. But don't write them as instructions or steps; write the values you are trying to move towards in your life and how this idea will move you one step closer. Getting too focused on specifics, pushes out the unexpected, which may be even better than what you were thinking.

I have so many ideas that I am almost overwhelmed. I have to force myself to stop! This isn't a race. Life isn't about money, popularity, or achievements. Life is about learning to love more deeply. **Am I doing that?** How did I grow in my giving of love today? How have I gone beyond me? Have I quieted myself down enough for God to give me insights? This is the most essential part of writing a journal. God needs you to slow down, reflect, and ponder. That's the time he will quietly inject His love and guidance into your life.

So you don't have a journal, yet. Start your first entry. You've just read about the concept. Don't repeat it. Write what moves you. Write about whatever the direction you want to go at this point in your life. Write about your goals and your dreams. Just do it. I promise I won't peek. Months and years down the road, you'll be glad you wrote down your thoughts and feelings.

Me and my life - right now:

____

____

____

____

____

____

____

Words Matter

Life is a communications blitz. Most of us interact with family, co-workers, and even strangers every day. The following is an essay that just poured out. I wasn't expecting it. But I think it fits at this point in the book.

It's 3 in the morning. It would be impeccably silent if it weren't for the waves of wind roaring through the trees. We all need that quiet time daily. Usually, I know where I am going when I write, but despite the stillness, my mind is yelling – write. So here goes!

Our relationships with those around us are built or destroyed by the words we use. Yes, actions are in there, but words are the control buttons. Life is complex. It needs to be. If it were boring, we wouldn't be challenged to grow. Every obstacle/event that happens to us challenges us to a new understanding of this world – of ourselves. **Words matter.** Words are how we interpret our inner being in relationship to this particular event, today – at this moment. Words are abstractions that represent our emotions and understanding of life. We may have deep sadness or overwhelming joy. It comes out in words. We can't mind-meld to share what is going on with someone else. So we use words; some are verbal and some are invisible in our body language.

Words matter. With them, you can destroy another person or elate another. It may be your partner, your kids, your parents, your friends, or your boss. Every relationship is molded by the words that come out of our mouths. I have talked about "speaking from the heart." That's where thoughts and emotions mix together and pour into this world. But you need to be in control! **Words matter!** When we verbalize our frustration with others, it will trigger negative things in them. Some reactions may be visible as a backlash. More importantly, your frustration may also cause irreversible damage to the other's heart or sense of worth in a fragile and demanding world.

You may be angry with your boss – **they have feelings.** They may feel inadequate in leading your team through tough times. They have struggles in their personal lives that may be surfacing in how they relate to you. Same with your partner or kids. We are all struggling through life, trying to figure out each moment. Planning ahead is only marginally crucial because, life just throws stuff at us. Didn't see that coming! Ponder those words. Are they building a relationship or destroying it? **Words matter.**

A second thought about words: **this is more fun.** Words express power! Surely you have been around someone who bores you. Others you can't wait to engage with. Many times, it isn't that one person is better than the other; it's just their skill at using words. I have met and talked with thousands of people. I hate small talk! Express who you are. Show me that you know who you are! When I was dating, I often asked them to tell me who they are early on. They would start telling me about their education or job. I would stop them and point out that is what they do. Tell me who you are! Many couldn't. It's time to move on. Those who had stopped long enough to really search for how to answer that question usually turned into friends or at least valued people. It isn't so much what they said; it was a connection at the heart level. Of course, I also had to be willing to open up at that level.

Words matter! I keep returning back to that because we throw words around with such carelessness that we fail to consider the impact on others. Reports are that 50% of teenage girls have considered suicide. Is it because the connectivity of cell phones in their lives allows mean words to be thrown out – words you would probably never say to someone's face? Partly! Are you choosing words that build relationships – partner, friends, kids? Or are you sabotaging that connection? I choose to love you, even if I haven't met you – yet. That is an internal choice I make each day. I don't know what is going to cross my path. I can't control most things in life. The challenge is to learn how to forgive, love, and understand others and myself daily. Choose your words wisely – **Words matter!**

What makes a good life?

What you consider a good life will change as you mature and go through the stages of life. If you grew up with little money, maybe making money is your goal. Finding peace or a quality relationship may be your goal if your family was dysfunctional.

However there are some key personality traits I would suggest you consider.

1. Am I honest?
2. Do I follow through with what I say I will do?
3. Can I be trusted?
4. Do I value other people and treat them with kindness?
5. Do I avoid gossip?

I'm sure there are many more qualities.

Your kids want to be just like you. If they see you being a good person, they will imitate you and want to be that kind of person. If you become the person you want your kids to be....

Trust is always at the top of my list. Do you do what you say you will do? Do you keep those promises? Can your family depend on you? You took a vow! Stick to it. Even trusting a spouse and not jumping to conclusions can keep many issues from turning into battles. Your kids love you and want to see a relationship between you and your spouse that works. They will model that in their own life someday. Even though partners and spouses don't always work out, how you handle the breakup disappointment directly reflects who you really are.

Your kid's future

Let go. Getting your kids into some Ivy League college isn't a guarantee to their happiness. Neither is finding the perfect partner for them mean happiness. Giving them a job in the family business doesn't allow them to prove themselves in the real world. Your kids were born with their own spirit. Their happiness will come when they have had time for free play as a child and also a free choice in determining their future. As a parent, they want to know that you love and support them - no strings attached. Sometimes life crushes their spirit, and they need to run home again, but it's their life, and they have to deal with it. They will make mistakes. Love them. They will fail. Love them. They will be too busy to visit. Love them. They will find their way. It won't be your way, but it has to be their choice. **Love them.**

Here is that action page again... How are you going to implement these ideas into your relationships?

Spouse:

Kids:

Friends:

As an Adult, You need to Play too!

We live in a high stress world. There are deadlines, financial pressures, and never enough time. You also need to rediscover play. Your mind and body needs to be active without a specific goal. Do something just because you feel like doing it.

- Soak up some sunshine.
- Lay in the grass and look for shapes in the clouds.
- Feel the breeze.
- Daydream. Ask yourself "What if..."
- Walk down a beach, feeling the sand between your toes.

Learning to play is powerful. Playing to learn is everything. Once you understand how it works, you can see its effect on you and your kids. Learn how to encourage free play. Make your environment and your trips into adventures. Embrace the discovery!

I truly believe that free play is the greatest gift we have all been given. The baby was born with it. Kids instinctively know what it is. It can be a lifelong friend that keeps us laughing and learning. Don't stop the magic. It's your best friend!

In every real man a child is hidden that wants to play

~ Friedrich Nietzsche

Paradise is a place where you play forever

~ *Annonymous*

Man is most nearly himself when he achieves the seriousness of a child at play

~ *Heraclitus*

Play is the royal road to childhood happiness and adult brilliance

~ *Joseph Chilton Pearce*

A little nonsense now and then
is cherished by the wisest men
~ Roald Dahl

Those who play rarely become brittle
in the face of stress or lose the
healing capacity for humor
~ Dr Stuart Brown, MD

Play keeps us vital and alive.
It gives us an enthusiasm for life
that is irreplaceable. Without it,
life just doesn't taste good
~ Lucia Capocchione

Tell yourself about your next adventures.

The Wrap Up

Several years ago, my wife and I were strolling down the middle of the street during a festival in Wooster, Ohio. There were vendors all around with beautiful artwork and handmade items. A live "Big Band" started playing – just the right tempo. Cindy and I wrapped an arm around each other's waist and started doing a kind of dance as we walked. With each step, we crossed our leg in front of the other person like we were just one person, in perfect sync. It was terrific fun as we kinda danced our way to the music. **People started pointing, laughing, trying to imitate us.** We were playing, having an unexpected free play. We really didn't care what others thought. It was fun!

Hopefully, you've read through most of this book and not just skipped to the end thinking I would summarize it so you wouldn't have to read the book. I can't do it. Only when you reflect on your upbringing, your play experiences can you begin to see how life-giving play is – no matter what age.

You may have discovered how your brain processes information. Perhaps you found that stepping into an argument between kids doesn't solve the problem. Perhaps you found that taking risks is essential or not every toy is "good". Maybe taking your kids to the local playground won't solve their "boredom." Are you going to be a "Storyteller" now? Are you seriously looking at how your kids are doing in the public school system? How many AH-HA moments did you have as you read through this book?

Dr. Gray in the Prologue to his book "Free to Learn," shares his wake up call when his 9 year old son Scott was in the school office, **again**. He couldn't do public school anymore! He wanted out! In dismay they pulled him out and searched for an alternative. They found a Sudbury School that fit him perfectly. He was in his element. But Dr. gray was experiencing a wake-up call in his own life. He realized that the school system was no longer working. He changed his life focus from biopsychology to the study of the educational system and how we learn. (That's my simplified assessment). He now does Tedtalks, podcasts and regular posts about how kids learn and how the "system" is failing them.

If your kids are struggling in the system, PLEASE, get them out! Their desire to learn is the most important ingredient in their life.

Hopefully this book will alter your family's path. Are you just following the crowd, or are you loving your kids to the point of risking a different path?

Understanding the importance of play in the learning process is one of the most important insights into life. To me, each day is an adventure unfolding. Who will cross my path and share a thought that changes me? Will a book title catch my eye? Will YouTube throw a suggested video that takes me down an unexpected exploration? My learning didn't stop at 6th grade, 12th grade, or a college degree. I try every day to learn something new, beyond my current skill set. I can see the big picture. I've also noticed that my life has changed since I started exploring how play works. I find myself lightening up and being joyful. I can't wait for each day to unfold. There is anticipation of the unknown. What an adventure!

We don't stop playing because we grow old;
we grow old because we stop playing
~ George Bernard Shaw

About the Author and Illustrator

About the author: He can't stop creating. Steve Andrews has a minor in Architecture and a major in Industrial Arts Education from Kent State University. He has taught design, drafting, graphic arts, metalworking, and home repairs, led youth groups, designed and built beautiful wooden toys and puppets, and has been a farmer. in 1979 he started a quick printing business, which he still runs.

His passions include showing kids how chicks are hatched, building Discovery Park Ohio, and writing about the value of free play. He was an early adopter in the homeschooling movement with his two kids and co-led hundreds of families in the early days. He dreams vividly and follows through with those dreams. Every day is a new adventure unfolding with wonderful people with whom to cross paths.

His wife, Cindy Farmer, the illustrator, has the gift of an artist's eye and the heart of an angel. She graduated from Columbus College of Art and has been sharing her gift with the world ever since. She raised four kids by doing art shows and festivals and continues expanding her art skills. She has illustrated this book with all the insights of watching thousands of kids on our playground.

Cindy is also a naturopathic consultant and can look at your iris and identify the health of every system in your body. She has written and illustrated a children's book about nutrition. Cindy has been a Tai Chi and Qi Gong instructor for many years.

Together, they have hosted, at their farm, over 50 young adults from around the world and daily seek to build a world that inspires others.

If someone were to invite you to be on a podcast, what would be your story?

About the reader:

Bibliography

At the end of most non-fiction books is a section that references all the books the author researched to write their book.

Here is my Journey...

I remember my tire swing and a giant sandbox when I was 5. When I turned 6, we moved, and the school playground was only a block away. It had swings, teeter totters, sand, and a ball field. The best part was a swamp in the far corner and the surrounding woods. In the summer, we would pack a lunch and head out to the woods to explore and build almost daily.

I studied architecture at Kent State University, and every project I would draw had a play area designed into it. I couldn't explain it. It just felt right, no matter what the assignment was. In those early years of my life, I stumbled across three books about playgrounds (the first three are on the following list). The summer of 1972, I worked at Cedar Point Amusement Park as a River Boat Captain. I loved it! It combined storytelling, adventure and some surprises, like drunken riders and boats running out of gas mid-journey. I also got to see the workings of an amusement park from the inside. But amusement parks are entertainment and not play.

Hindsight is an excellent teacher. I now know that my heart has wanted to be focused on how play is essential to our lives. So, here are the books that have helped me on this journey.

Book 1: ***Design for Play*** by Richard Dattner AIA (American Institute of Architects) 1969 by Reinhart Book Corporation

This is a rather academic study of playgrounds around the world. What struck me most was the author's analysis of the development of play as a child grows. Like any good architect, he points out that great play spaces have to involve those who will use the space in the planning process.

Book 2: ***Playgrounds for Free*** by Paul Hogan 1974 by MIT Press

Book 3: ***The Nuts and Bolts of Playground Construction*** by Paul Hogan 1982 Leisure Press

These two books by the same author are amazing. This man worked with groups and communities to design and build over 350 play spaces worldwide. He didn't believe a government-provided play space had any value. He brought kids and families together to create the kind of play THEY wanted. He was a facilitator who taught them how to think, work together, and build their own space.

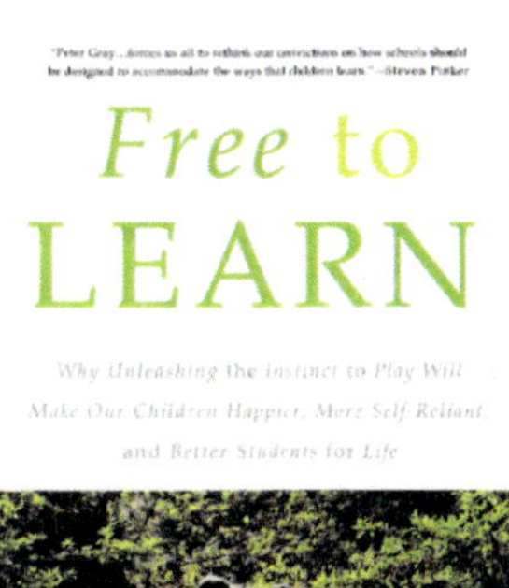

Book 4: ***Free to Learn*** by Peter Gray 2013 Basic Books.

Dr. Gray's book has helped me in every way to understand all the interactions I see on my playground. **If you want to understand play even more, this is the one book to start your journey.** Thank you, Dr. Gray, for the gift you have given us. Every parent needs to read this book and watch his videos and interviews.

Book 5: ***How Children Fail*** by John Holt 1964 DaCuPo Press

Book 6: ***How Children Learn*** by John Holt 1967 DaCuPo Press

Book 7: ***Learning All the Time*** by John Holt 1989 Perseus Books

Most of us went through the public school system. We are the survivors. John Holt has shared his insights through millions of books worldwide. His insights into the failures of the learning process struck a deep chord in me. If you want to understand your kids and how they REALLY learn, you should read these books.

Book 8: ***Until the Streetlights Come On*** by Ginny Yurich, M.Ed. 2023 Baker Books

I've met Ginny. She gets it. Home-schooling 5 of her own kids after spending 10 years teaching math in "the system," she gets it. 10 years ago, she started "1000 Hours Outside". She understands that play isn't about toys; it's about discovery. She gets it!

Book 9: ***Simplicity Parenting*** by Kim John Payne, M.Ed.2010 Ballantine Books

Kim John Payne teaches us how to simplify our lives so we have less conflict and more time for each other. This leads to Calmer, Happier, and More Secure Kids.

NOTES

1 Page 17 Free to LEARN page 122
2 Page 20 Free to LEARN page 142
3 Page 24 Free to LEARN page 147
4 Page 48 Free to LEARN page 171
5 Page 59 Simplicity Parenting page 60
6 Page 62 Free to LEARN page 163
7 Page 74 Free to LEARN page 138
8 Page 74 Learning all the Time page 4
9 Page 83 Until the Streetlights Come On page 93
10 Page 107 Free to LEARN page 50
11 Page 109 Free to LEARN page 174

CHILDREN

And a woman who held a babe against her bosom said,
Speak to us of children.
And he said:
Your children are not your children.
They are the sons and daughters of Life's longing for itself.
They come through you but not from you.
And though they are with you yet they belong not to you.
You may give them your love but not your thoughts.
You may house their bodies but not their souls,
For their souls dwell in the house of tomorrow, which you cannot visit, not even in your dreams.
You may strive to be like them, but seek not to make them like you.
For life goes not backward nor tarries with yesterday.
You are the bows from which your children as living arrows are sent forth.
The archer sees the mark upon the path of the infinite, and He bends you with His might that His arrows may go swift and far.
Let your bending in the Archer's hand be for gladness;
For even as He loves the arrow that flies, so He loves also the bow that is stable.

Kahlil Gibran

Kahlil is best known as the author of The Prophet, which was first published in the United States in 1923 and has since become one of the best-selling books of all time, having been translated into more than 100 languages.

WOW

Thank you for reading my book. You're a part of a special group. I am told that only 20% of people who start reading a book actually finish it. You made it! I hope this book was everything I promised it would be and that ideas have already started percolating in your head that will bring more joy to your family.

Please help this book reach more people by going to Amazon and giving an honest review of this book.

It's wild that we live in such a shady world that we don't buy or deal with someone until we've read many reviews. So, if this book resonates with you, please share it on my review page. If something here doesn't feel right, don't be afraid to say that. I'm not perfect. If you have areas you think should be explored more, share them too. There will probably be an updated version later.

If you would like bulk copies of this book to share with friends or want to have a book club reading, write to me at steph@camelotprinting.com for discounted prices. I'm also a printer and I can produce my books in my print shop next door.

Search for my author page on Amazon and you will discover other books I have or am writing. I have many other books swirling in my head, just waiting for some daylight.